AWKWARD AWAKENING

For more information, visit the author's website:
angelintraining.org

Scott Guerin Publishing
Stewartsville, New Jersey
SG-Publishing.com
guerinscott@gmail.com

Cover and interior design by Hailee Pavey
Pavey Design | paveydesign.com

ISBN: 979-8-9990391-2-5
Library of Congress Control Number: 2025919678

COVER

In many of the ancient temples in Egypt, on the doorway going into the Holy of Holies, a site's most sacred room, the word *SABA* is embedded on the frame. Two symbols of the word *SABA*, which means "gateway to the stars," are used in the cover design of this book: the rectangle with an extra line on the top and sides refers to a gateway, and the star with the dot at its center signifies a civilization.

PRAISE FOR
AWKWARD AWAKENING

Dr. Guerin uses a blend of science and intuitive spirituality to guide readers through the awakening process and our divine nature, while outlining humanity's next developmental step—contact with our galactic family. He empowers readers by reminding them that the answers lie within, encouraging a return to the eternal state of consciousness that connects us all, which we refer to as Love.

—*Melissa Sparrow, light worker, healer, and medium*

Awkward Awakening is an honest, vulnerable, and brilliantly woven exploration of consciousness and cosmic connection. Dr. Guerin bridges science and spirit with rare clarity and courage—guiding readers through the messy, miraculous process of awakening to who we truly are.

—*Nichole Bigley, founder and CEO of AudioWakes, coauthor of* **Looking for Angels,** *and host of* **A Psychic's Story** *podcast*

Awkward Awakening is a clear and compelling journey of personal transformation. Dr. Guerin connects the physical with the metaphysical, emphasizing that doing the internal work to align with higher frequencies brings us closer to the state of Oneness already realized by civilizations throughout the galaxy. Despite its vast scope, the book conveys big ideas with Guerin's signature clarity and brevity and provides steps to continue our journey of self-discovery.

—*Michael R. Kandel, PsyD*

FINDING
YOUR
WAY
HOME

AWKWARD
AWAKENING

SCOTT GUERIN, PhD

NOTE TO THE READER

This book is best viewed as a primer. It discusses many topics, all with implications for life and spiritual awakening. While background information and research on many of the subjects could easily fill a small library, footnotes have been minimized to make this book more readable. You will find citations for quoted material, along with suggested readings for each chapter, in the back of the book so that you can dive deeper into any topics that interest you.

Your journey is just beginning!

Terms

Some of the many terms used throughout this book have different meanings or connotations depending upon the context. The following definitions are intended to clarify the meaning of these terms as used in this book.

God/Source encompasses all ideas of the Divine, God, and all the names used to describe this concept.

ETs denotes extraterrestrial beings in general.

Star Nations, galactic neighbors, galactic neighborhoods, galactic brothers and *sisters,* and *galactic families* all refer to living beings from other worlds, star systems, or parts of the universe.

In this book, the terms *mind* and *consciousness* are used interchangeably. They both have connections to the physical body but are also nonphysical in nature.

Organized religion refers to any structured system of faith or worship, formal doctrines, rituals, methods of worship, or practices.

Finally, you do not have to believe or accept everything that is presented in this book or the words of the authors referenced. As I will discuss later, we all decide what we choose to believe. My recommendation is to take whatever content resonates with you and leave the rest for now.

Disclaimer

This book is designed to provide information and inspiration to its readers, with the understanding that the author does not intend to render any type of emotional, legal, medical, mental, psychological, religious, or any other kind of professional advice, nor prescribe the use of any technique or practice as a form of treatment. The author/publisher shall not be liable for any commercial, emotional, financial, physical, psychological, or spiritual damages, including but not limited to special, incidental, consequential, or other damages. The author/publisher and any other associated parties assume no responsibility for your actions and their consequences accrued from the information in this book.

Always consult a physician or therapist when considering using the techniques listed within this book. Always make sure to practice the meditations, intentions, prayers, or exercises in an environment that is safe to do so. Do not engage in these activities while driving a car or operating any kind of machinery.

WITH GRATITUDE

This book was given to me. I had a vague idea that it would be about awakening but didn't know much beyond that. During an Akashic record reading with psychic medium and energy healer Melissa Sparrow, it became clear that the book was going to be written. Melissa told me, "They're saying it's meant to reach those who are on the cusp or in the beginning of their awakening journey. Your book is going to assist individuals and practitioners in that journey, support them, guide them, and give them the tools they need." I was also told that it was going to be galactic in nature. I was unsure of what that meant at the time.

I am deeply grateful to my spirit guides, angels, Mom and Dad, and ETs for their guidance and encouragement throughout the writing process. It was quite an experience. I am so thankful for my wife, Debbie, for putting up with a distracted, often detached writer who needed to "come back to Earth" at times. The person who introduced me to the celestial realm in a practical, honest, and safe way, igniting my exploration, is guide and author Marty Rawson, whose work I am honored to present in Chapter 16. I owe an enormous amount of thanks to Brian Patterson and Dr. Michael Kandel for their valuable insights in reading the first drafts of the manuscript. Special thanks to Melissa Wallace for her eagle eye and expert insights. Each of you played an important role in sharing your perspectives and confirming that I was on the right track. Last, but not least, I feel so blessed to be able to work with designer Hailee Pavey and editor Susan Davidson in the development of this book. These two talented and brilliant ladies are the best in the business.

And to you, the reader, this is for you. The awakening process may be unsettling at first and will require some work on your part. But the result will transform your life into an incredible and exciting journey.

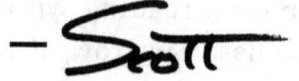

— Scott

"Aunt Em, is that you? I must have had a dream, but it was so real!"

—*Dorothy,* **The Wizard of Oz** *(1939), MGM Studios*

CONTENTS

SECTION 1
A STARTING POINT

SECTION 2
AWAKENING TO WHO WE REALLY ARE

SECTION 3
AWAKENING TO OUR PLACE
IN THE UNIVERSE

INTRODUCTION

Things are about to change.

As strange as it seems, we are waking up.

Some spiritually minded people are familiar with spiritual awakening and have an idea of what is to come. However, for many of you, this idea and the related metaphysical concepts and sources are new and may cause you some concern, even fear.

This book can be a help to you by taking you step-by-step through two significant developments related to the process of awakening in humanity: the first is the connection to our divine nature and one another. This will trigger the second development: open contact with our ET neighbors. As you learn about these civilizations you may be surprised that they feel familiar and remind you of a far-away Home.

As with almost every major innovation or discovery, this awakening will be met with resistance, because it will mean that many of our beliefs about the physical and nonphysical worlds must change. Some information comes from traditional sources, and other content comes from places that might seem strange to you. If you keep an open mind and seriously consider this material, you will glean valuable insights and strategies to help you prepare for the transformation, offering you hope and a way to actively participate.

There have been other paradigm shifts in human history—those related to scientific breakthroughs, expanded communication, and social and political movements. Each of them has had a substantial impact on our world.

This shift is going to be bigger than all of them.

A STARTING POINT

CHAPTER ONE

AWAKENING TO
A PARADIGM SHIFT

"All great truths begin as blasphemies."
—*George Bernard Shaw*

A fundamental aspect of awakening is accepting change. The fact that we are awakening means that we are encountering something new, and humans tend to resist new ideas. This is especially true for groups and organizations, such as businesses, religions, and universities. These groups have invested substantial time and resources in building the infrastructure supporting their ideas. When contradictory theories or ideas are presented, they may be met with significant resistance because the groups are attempting to preserve their organizational culture, beliefs, and, often, income.

While most of the information presented in this book is *not* new—much of it has been known for decades or even thousands of years—what *is* new is that we are rapidly approaching a flash point of awareness about Who we really are and our place in the universe. Both of these ideas will be resisted.

To give you an idea of how society reacts to change, let's take a trip back in time to sixteenth-century Poland. For years a young man walked along a beach at night, looking up at the tapestry of the sky he knew so well. But much as he tried, he could not rid himself of the thought that something was wrong. He had an idea that went against everything he had learned about the sun, moon, and stars—that all celestial bodies revolved around Earth—knowledge handed down by intellectual giants like Aristotle and Ptolemy. The seat of the scientific community at the time, the Catholic Church, also backed this Earth-centered model of the universe.

But a handful of unblinking stars puzzled the Polish man so much that it robbed him of a restful night's sleep for months. These stars wandered about the night sky, not following any pattern and certainly not tracking around Earth like the other celestial bodies he observed.

Then it came to him.

Perhaps it was divine inspiration or a vision in a dream, but he conceived of an explanation for the stars' movement that made sense. Weeks of intense study confirmed his observations. A part of him must have wanted to be wrong— it would have been so much easier—but at the same time, he felt compelled to share what he knew, no matter the cost. And the cost would be great.

The young man was, of course, Nicolaus Copernicus, a mathematician, astronomer, physician, and economist born in the late 1400s in Poland. He must have struggled for years to solve the cosmic puzzle he observed, and he was undoubtedly hesitant to share his eventual discovery that the sun was the center of a solar system, with the Earth and moon rotating around it, along with other celestial bodies he called "wanderers" (based on the Greek word *planētēs*). The ridicule, rejection, and personal pain he must have felt as the scientific community—which, at that time, was the Catholic Church—and most likely, his friends, family, and colleagues, condemned his ideas could only have been devastating.

Copernicus knew his ideas would elicit a strong reaction from the Church, so he waited until he was on his deathbed in May 1543, at the age of seventy, to publish a book on his theory, *On the Revolutions of the Heavenly Spheres.* As anticipated, his work was met with severe resistance. Almost sixty years later, in 1600, the Italian philosopher Giordano Bruno was burned at the stake by the Roman Inquisition for his support of Copernicus's theory, in addition to other ideas deemed heretical. It took another thirteen years for Galileo Galilei to openly express support for the Copernican sun-centered system in *Letters on Sunspots.* Twenty years after that, Galileo was convicted of heresy by the Church; he spent the rest of his life under house arrest. Not until 1992, 359 years later, did the Vatican formally acknowledge that it had made a mistake in condemning Galileo.

"Sometimes people don't want to hear the truth because they don't want their illusions destroyed."
—*Friedrich Nietzsche*

Copernicus's experience was not unique. Other significant paradigm shifts in human history—such as the discovery that the Earth was not flat, the germ theory of disease, and the development of quantum mechanics—have also been met with initial rejection.

Why Humans Resist Change

When a new idea is presented, especially one that challenges current beliefs, it is often dismissed. Three psychological theories explain why this happens: cognitive dissonance, psychological inertia, and change theory.

"All truth passes through three stages. First, it is ridiculed. Second, it is violently opposed. Third, it is accepted as being self-evident."

—*Arthur Schopenhauer*

COGNITIVE DISSONANCE

When presented with conflicting or competing ideas, the emotional tension we feel is called "cognitive dissonance." The intensity of our discomfort varies depending on how important the conflicting ideas are to us. It is possible to reduce dissonant feelings in three ways.

First, we can change our attitude about what is being resisted by simply accepting the new idea. Second, we can seek information supporting the new idea, obtaining sufficient evidence to alleviate the tension we feel from the conflicting concepts. For example, after reading *On the Revolutions of the Heavenly Spheres,* Copernicus's contemporaries might initially have been upset by his revolutionary ideas. However, by studying his observations and speaking with other astronomers, they could have gained confidence in his new solar system model, eliminating their dissonant feelings. Third, and most common, we can trivialize and dismiss the conflicting attitudes or behaviors. In 1543 many people simply rejected the ideas presented by Copernicus because they were new, controversial, and not accepted by scientific leaders.

PSYCHOLOGICAL INERTIA

Another reason people reject new ideas is psychological inertia. This is a combination of several psychological phenomena, including fear of the unknown, habit, routine, social pressure, and emotional attachment. When a person in a new job asks why something is done a certain way and is met with the response, "That's the way we have always done it," that is psychological inertia. This approach is certainly easier than grappling with new ideas because we don't have to justify, investigate, or rationalize anything; it's the "if it ain't broke, don't fix it" mentality. Copernicus's contemporaries might have thought, "If the Earth-centered solar system was good enough for Aristotle, Ptolemy, and other scientists, it's good enough for me." Overcoming psychological inertia can take a lot of work and time, especially for those who do not like change or have an open mind.

> "All truth passes through three stages. First, it is
> ridiculed. Second, it is violently opposed.
> Third, it is accepted as being self-evident."
> —Arthur Schopenhauer

CHANGE THEORY

Change theory can also be used to explain humans' reluctance to accept new ideas. At one point in my career, I worked for a large behavioral health company. One of the services we provided was conducting training for corporate clients. The most requested training topic was how to manage change. Our clients would ask us to help their employees accept changes in the workplace, from learning a new computer system to relocating their department or adjusting to a new parking garage.

There are several change management theories, but the company I worked for chose to treat change as a loss and guide employees through the five stages of grief, originally developed by Elisabeth Kübler-Ross in her 1969 book *On Death and Dying*. In this model, change is the loss of something familiar, whether we liked it or not. That loss launches us through the five stages of grief: denial, anger, bargaining, depression, and acceptance.

It is important to note that we do not always go through the stages of grief in a linear fashion. Denial and anger are most prevalent at the onset of a big change, but we can revisit these early stages as we continue to process and engage with change.

As Copernicus's sun-centered theory worked its way through scientific and religious communities over the decades following its publication, their members most likely experienced each stage of grief. It can be overwhelming to consider a huge departure from a scientific theory established centuries before and supported by virtually all the pillars of knowledge. However, changes of this magnitude have occurred throughout history, along with the requisite opposition. I believe the coming awakening will meet just as much, if not more, resistance.

CHAPTER TWO

THE UNSEEN WORLD

"A man's got to know his limitations."
—Magnum Force *(1973)*

Awakening begins when we realize there is something out there beyond what we know and can comprehend.

As you are able to, stop reading this book and become aware of your surroundings. You might hear sounds of nature, traffic, children playing, or a television in the background. You might have thoughts about where you are, what you have to do by the end of the day, whether a storm is coming, or what you will have for lunch.

From a strictly biological perspective, the brain is encased in darkness and only receives information through five sensory inputs. This means we move through the world with a set of microphones, cameras, and other sensors that feed information to our brain, which, in turn, processes the inputs and, along with memory, creates what we perceive as reality.

Our sensory inputs are limited, however. The human eye can only perceive the frequency of physical light, but this is just .004 percent of the full electromagnetic energy spectrum bombarding us daily. We cannot see X-rays, ultraviolet light, radio waves, and more. Likewise, we can only hear sounds within a frequency range of about 20 to 20,000 Hz, which

"If you want to
find the secrets
of the universe,
think in terms of
energy, frequency,
and vibration."

—*Nikola Tesla*

is very limited compared to other life forms (see Figure 1). This means we are largely unaware of an enormous amount of activity around us, including an unseen world of energy, other dimensions, and entities that lie beyond the limits of our senses.

Conventional science does not have many answers about the unseen world; however, physicists are able to provide the beginnings of an explanation of how the spirit world may work.

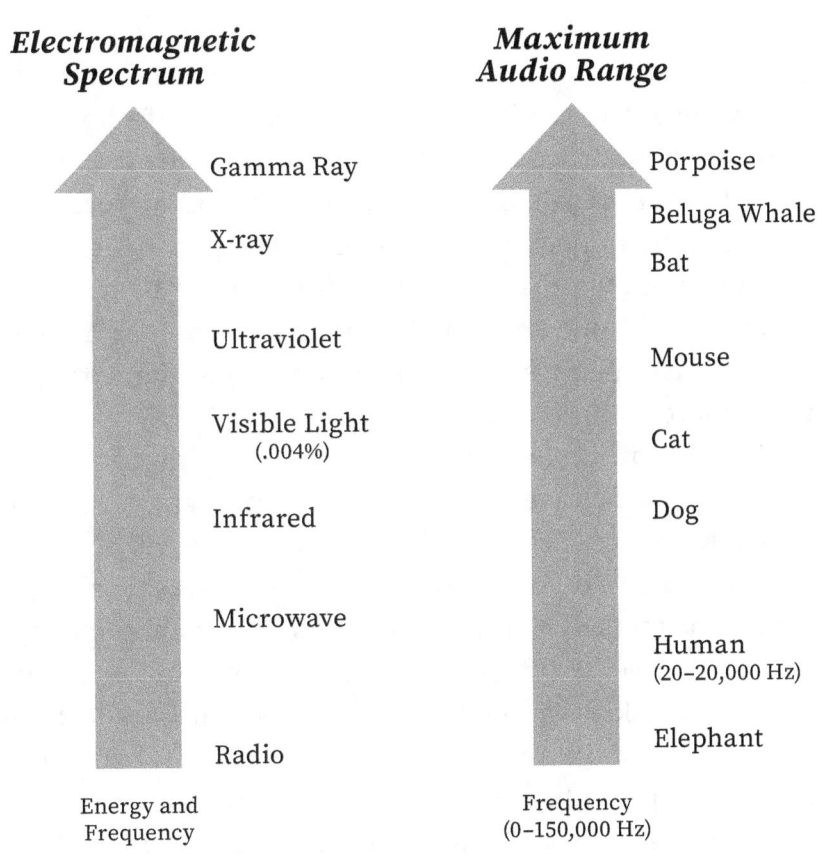

Figure 1. Human electromagnetic and audio capabilities.

Good Vibrations

One new way we are learning to understand the interaction between the seen and unseen worlds is through vibrations. Everything in our world is made up of energy vibrating at specific frequencies. For example, humans are made up of cells, which are made up of atoms, which are made up of particles, which are all vibrating energy.

"If you want to find the secrets of the universe, think in terms of energy, frequency, and vibration."
—*Nikola Tesla*

The speed of vibrating particles impacts our life in many ways, whether we realize it or not. We also have the ability to consciously modify our vibrational levels. For example, different types of music can influence our mood, we can pick up on positive or negative vibes from others, and vibrational vortices of energy that align with parts of the body, called chakras, affect our emotional and physical health. Ancient practices like yoga are meant to help adjust misaligned vibrational energy.

From a spiritual/emotional perspective, higher vibrational frequencies are associated with love, light, and unity, while lower frequencies are linked to anger, hatred, and separation. The Law of Attraction (LoA)—the universal principle that like attracts like—is a good way to identify and manage vibrational levels. Motivational speakers and authors Esther and Jerry Hicks, who developed hundreds of publications and resources on the LoA—Abraham-Hicks[1]—explained, "Every thought vibrates, every thought radiates a signal, and every thought attracts a matching signal back."[2] They used the example of a radio tower transmitting a signal at a specific frequency. When the transmitter and receiver are mismatched, nothing happens, but when they are in alignment, the signal flows. So it is with our thoughts; whatever we give our conscious attention to emits a vibration that attracts the object of our thoughts. In this way, we create the world we are experiencing.

To help illuminate our emotions, the Hickses identified emotions as a sixth sense—like taste, touch, smell, sight, and hearing. Our emotional vibrational levels relate to Who we are at our deepest levels, rather than being limited to our physical experiences. In order to use this sixth sense to influence the LoA, we must first become aware of our emotional levels and then develop the ability to change them to align with what we want to do, be, or have. In their book *Ask and It Is Given,* the Hickses provided twenty-two ways to change the vibrational signal we are emitting in any given moment, based on our thoughts, emotions, and beliefs. They identify these signals as our "point of attraction" or "set point." We can change our signals by visualizing what we want and monitoring and changing our feelings to align with our vision.[3] To help with this process, they offer emotional descriptions to enable us to precisely identify how we are feeling in the moment, ranging from the highest, most positive emotions (joy, knowledge, empowerment, freedom, love, and appreciation) to the lowest (fear, grief, depression, despair, and powerlessness).

As you would guess, verifying the LoA with a scientific method is difficult because assessing a person's vibrational level in relation to a target desire is complicated. Also, any doubts or contradictory feelings are hard to control for in study designs.

Finally, from a practical perspective, spiritual beings like angels, ghosts, ETs, and those who have passed vibrate at very high vibrational levels, making them invisible to the

Spiritual beings vibrate at very high vibrational levels, making them invisible to the human eye. Imagine a fan. When it is not running, we can easily see the blades; however, when the blades start spinning, they become invisible.

human eye and most present-day detection devices. Imagine a fan. When it is not running, we can easily see the blades; however, when the blades start spinning, they become invisible. Likewise, we can only see spiritual beings when they slow their vibrational speed to match ours. They are able to vary the vibrational rate of the molecules in their body (or the image of their body). We don't know how, but we hope to learn more about this in the future.

Quantum Insights

Quantum physics provides insight into the unseen world, shedding light on how the quantum world operates beyond the scope of classical physics. For example, in the sub-atomic/quantum realm, objects can exist in multiple states simultaneously and can instantly interact across great distances in addition to being influenced simply by observation. Albert Einstein was aware of this interconnection between atomic particles and described it as "spooky action at a distance."[4]

Just as we can change our vibrational levels to impact our emotions and attractions, our thoughts can impact the physical world as well. For example, the "observer effect" demonstrates that particles behave differently when they are observed, meaning that we can influence the physical world through our thoughts. Dr. Joe Dispenza—a neuroscientist, chiropractor, and best-selling author—has conducted numerous studies showing that by shifting their focus and emotional state, a person can alter their physical body.[5] We will discuss how this can happen in more detail in Chapter 8.

Regarding how our brains experience consciousness, a recent study conducted by Professor Mike Wiest at Wellesley College in Massachusetts provided support to the theory of the quantum basis of consciousness. His research focused on microtubules, which are part of neurons in the brain and identified as possible areas that enable quantum processes. In examining how anesthesia affects the brain, Wiest and his research team worked with rats and a microtubule-binding drug. The results showed that the drug interfered with the anesthesia. Wiest stated that since classical perspectives do not explain this interference, "this finding supports the quantum model of consciousness."[6]

Quantum physics does not prove the unseen worlds of angels, nonphysical entities, or ETs, but it does crack open the door from the mechanistic world of classical physics, shedding light on new discoveries in the unseen world. Learning more about the power of the mind and how humans can interact with the physical and nonphysical worlds will be a large part of the awakening process. I believe we will make some of these discoveries on our own; however, we will also get help from other sources.

Where Does Your Mind Reside?

In order to awaken to Who we really are, we must determine where the mind resides, and whether "we," meaning the conscious awareness of ourselves, reside solely in our physical bodies or as some form of energy. Many theories have been developed and discarded over time; for this discussion, we will look at the two most prominent schools of thought. The first, physicalism, defines the mind solely as a result of neurological connections within the brain that translate and interpret inputs from sensory receptors and memory. The other perspective, dualism, acknowledges that the mind and the phenomenon of consciousness are beyond the brain. This means that some mental processes extend beyond the nervous system and reside somewhere outside of the body, suggesting a yet-to-be-understood explanation for how the mind works.

The physicalist perspective appeals to many people because neurological processes are "scientific," meaning they are observable and measurable (scientific materialism). However, as the famed Swiss psychiatrist and psychoanalyst Carl Jung noted, "We must completely give up the idea of the psyche's being somehow connected with the brain."[7] He believed in the existence of angels and other nonphysical aspects of our reality, and focused much of his work on the spiritual world. He understood the dangers of viewing the world as solely material or mechanistic, stating:

> Under the influence of scientific materialism, everything that could not be seen with the eyes or touched with the hands was held in doubt. Such things were even laughed at for their supposed affinity with metaphysics. Nothing was considered to be scientific or admitted to be true unless it could be perceived by the sense or traced back to a physical being.[8]

Since Jung's time, researchers have studied mind-body connection, mind-matter interaction, consciousness, and the connection between quantum mechanics and consciousness, also known as parapsychology (psi). I spent two years studying these topics for my doctoral dissertation, "The Effects of Prayer on the Quality of Life in Older Adults" (The Fielding Graduate University, 2005). It is clear that the human mind is more than just physical material operating electronically; it can significantly impact the physical world. However, the research does not offer a consistent explanation of *how* the mind causes these changes.

Dr. Gary Schwartz, a professor at the University of Arizona and director of the Laboratory for Advances in Consciousness and Health, has conducted extensive research on another aspect of consciousness: whether it can exist after death. In his book *The Afterlife Experiments*, he described how he tested mediums' ability to connect with people who have passed. The mediums in his study did not know the deceased subjects, nor had they been provided with any information about them. The details the mediums reported receiving were specific and statistically significant, suggesting that consciousness may persist after death.

While we perceive our physical world largely through our five senses, the nature of the mind is up for debate. Does it exist outside of the brain? Can it influence the material world around us? Although research provides an affirmative answer to both questions, it also suggests that we have a spiritual nature with unknown capabilities. As our awakening proceeds, we must seek out more information about ourselves and our world—whether through science, religious teachings, dreams, channeling, or other sources.

CHAPTER THREE

MODERN-DAY SOURCES

"The truth is rarely pure and never simple."
—*Oscar Wilde*

The elephant in the room in this discussion is where our information about the unseen world comes from and whether it can be trusted. Science can only take us so far and often lags behind experience because it is limited to subjects that can be observed and measured by our senses or instruments. Even with breakthrough discoveries in the quantum world, spiritual topics—such as spirits, angels, ETs, and even the nature of the mind—are still largely outside the grasp of scientific investigation.

How Do We Know What We Know?

The discipline of epistemology, which means "the theory of knowledge," includes many models for how we acquire knowledge. One popular model, comprising four methods for forming opinions, was introduced by Charles Sanders Peirce in 1877 in an essay titled "Fixation of Belief."[1] I have found this model to be helpful in explaining how we develop our beliefs about the unseen world.

The first method is *authority*. This is the primary way we learn as children, mainly from parents, teachers, and religious leaders. As we mature, we still rely on authority figures for information. We accept what they say simply because of who they are, without verification or validation. On the positive side, this is a simple way to learn; however, the value of the knowledge we gain depends on the reliability of the authority figure.

The second method is *tenacity*, or the assurance we have after first determining something to be true. Tenacity creates steadfastness in times of uncertainty or chaos, allowing us to find comfort in our knowledge and religious or spiritual beliefs. But because tenacity makes it very difficult to change our minds, even if new information is presented, we may reject any information that runs counter to our accepted worldview. Tenacity can also lead to prejudice, racism, and judgment.

The third method for forming beliefs is *scientific investigation*. This specifically refers to empirical science, meaning knowledge gained through observation, which is considered the most reliable way to learn about the world. The one significant drawback to scientific investigation is that a subject must be able to be observed and measured in some tangible way, as in a laboratory, in order for us to develop beliefs about it. Spiritual and otherwise nonphysical subjects are difficult, if not impossible, to study in a laboratory.

The fourth method is *a priori*. Beliefs developed in this way do not require any direct evidence, but are based on self-evident truths and even intuition. A priori beliefs can also develop when we have vast knowledge of a subject. For example, we may provide an answer to a question instantaneously, without knowing exactly how we came up with that answer.

"Again and again, some people in the crowd wake up. They carry strange customs with them, and demand room for bold gestures. The future speaks ruthlessly through them."
—*Rainer Maria Rilke*

A PRIORI SPIRITUAL BELIEFS

I have expanded the definition of a priori beliefs, recognizing that it encompasses all the ways we develop beliefs beyond the other three methods. It is important to consider other sources for our beliefs—from automatic writing and psychic abilities to dreams, channeling, and the deep trance state of hypnotic somnambulism—because they provide fundamental information about our physical and spiritual worlds and map out the next phase of humanity's growth.

Sacred Religious Texts

I once had an illuminating discussion with a man about angels, spirits, and deceased loved ones. He told me he did not believe in angels because they could not be scientifically proven. Earlier in the conversation, he had mentioned that he was a devout Catholic, so I felt I could challenge him a bit. I asked, "So, you don't believe in angels because they cannot be validated scientifically, but you believe in the virgin birth, resurrection, and forgiveness of sins without any evidence whatsoever?" We concluded that, for him, the evidence for these ideas was that they were all written about in a sacred book.

At first glance, religious texts could fall under the authority method of developing beliefs. After all, because they are the texts of a particular religion, their followers deem them to be true without question. I believe these religious texts are a priori because their sources and the nature of their transmission vary greatly and are nonphysical. The Ten Commandments and Code of Hammurabi were supposedly inscribed on stone tablets; the Book of Mormon was written on golden plates and delivered to Joseph Smith by the spirit Moroni. Other records of divine inspiration were conveyed through oral traditions or written on parchment paper or cave walls.

In each case, a human received information with their senses or mind, which they then recorded or shared orally. The first five books of the Hebrew Bible (Old Testament) are believed to have been authored by Moses or several authors who wrote under that name through divine inspiration. The Quran was verbally revealed to the Prophet Muhammad by the Archangel Gabriel. In the New Testament, the apostle Paul wrote that all scripture is inspired by God, or "God-breathed."

For some people strongly attached to their religion, the idea that sacred texts were, using the modern-day term, "channeled" through humans from divine sources may be off-putting. A critical part of the awakening process is to accept that God/Source communicates with us regularly through channeling and, in fact, has never stopped.

Automatic Writing

The phenomenon of automatic writing occurs when a person's hand starts to move on its own to record thoughts that do not originate from the person's mind. For example, Neale Donald Walsch, the author of the prolific *Conversations with God* series, was recording his frustrations and questions on a notepad one evening when his hand began writing answers to the questions he had posed. Likewise, Helen Schucman, the author of *A Course* in *Miracles*, explained that she received the book's content through a series of inner visions and hearing an inner voice directly from Jesus, like dictation.

This is a very common way for people to receive ideas from Spirit, and many claim that entire books were written using this method. In fact, I experience this at times as I write. Sometimes, as I'm developing a chapter or paragraph, concentrating on the best way to convey a thought, my mind will temporarily blank out for a few seconds, and I will realize that a paragraph or page has been written. When I read it back, I'll be amazed and say to myself, "This is brilliant; who wrote this?"

The Clairs

The clairs (from the French word for "clear") refer to the innate psychic abilities we all have that enable us to receive information beyond our physical senses. We all have one or two clairs that are most prominent, and some people have several. If you think you don't have any psychic abilities, I boldly assert that you are incorrect. I say this because two years ago, if anyone had asked if I had psychic abilities, I would have said, "Absolutely not." However, as I was working on *Looking for Angels* with Nichole Bigley and on her podcast, *A Psychic's Story*, I put in the time, effort, and intention to uncover my psychic abilities. To my great surprise, I have identified and seen a dramatic increase in my claircognizance and clairvoyance.

If you are interested in learning about your psychic abilities, set your intentions and spend some time investigating the eight different types of clairs: clairaudience (clear hearing), claircognizance (clear knowing), clairempathy (sensing others' emotions), clairgustance (clear tasting), clairintellect (clear thinking), clairsalience (clear smelling),

"The dream is
the small hidden
door in the deepest
and most intimate
sanctum of the soul."

—*Carl Jung*

clairsentience (clear physical feeling), and clairvoyance (clear seeing). You may be surprised what is shown to you. Once you identify one clair, keep noticing when it comes through. Your natural tendencies and sensitivities are also a way to deepen your spiritual connections and ignite a new part of your journey.

Dreams

Dreams are another powerful way we connect with Spirit and receive messages, visions, and guidance. When Nichole Bigley and I were writing *Looking for Angels,* we conducted a survey of people's thoughts about angels.[2] One of the survey questions asked if the participant had experienced an angelic encounter and provided a list of twelve types of angelic encounters. Of the almost eight hundred responses received, the most common type of angelic encounter that participants had experienced was "Having vivid or recurring dreams that feel different from other dreams."

> "The dream is the small hidden door in the deepest and most intimate sanctum of the soul."
> — *Carl Jung*

Many dreams are based on remnant thoughts and experiences from throughout the day. Others may be ongoing frustrations or fears we are working through. If you experience vivid dreams that seem out of the ordinary, they could very well be a message.

There are many examples of great artists and inventors who received world-changing information through their dreams. For example, Albert Einstein's famous equation $E=mc^2$ came to him in a dream in which he imagined himself riding a beam of light. Thomas Edison credited his discovery of electricity to his dreams. James Cameron said the idea for the movie *Avatar* came to him in a dream.

Channeling

There is a strong argument that all the a priori ways we receive information and develop beliefs fall under the umbrella term *channeling,* in which information is funneled or channeled to us from spiritual sources. Author Mike Dooley provided a wonderful definition of channeling in his book *The Great Awakening.* According to Dooley, channeling is "the ability to intentionally alter your conscious focus to allow the spiritual energy of another from this density, dimension, world, plane, or others to physically communicate through you, usually through writing or spoken word."[3] In this definition, Dooley emphasized the importance of allowing. From my experience, communication sometimes comes to us unannounced, which makes it all the more important for us to allow it in.

It is important to remember that we must be vigilant in pursuing the truth in love in any way we receive information. I like the definition of love found in the New Testament book of 1 Corinthians (13:4–7). I apply this definition to my own actions and evaluate others' speech and behavior based on these parameters:

> Love is patient, love is kind. It does not envy, it does not boast, it is not proud. It does not dishonor others, it is not self-seeking, it is not easily angered, it keeps no record of wrongs. Love does not delight in evil but rejoices with the truth. It always protects, always trusts, always hopes, always perseveres.

Dooley suggested that we evaluate the information we channel using three parameters: Does it speak of life's beauty? Does it speak of our power? Is it non-exclusionary, leaving no one behind?

Hypnosis

I include hypnosis in this section not because it is an a priori method of developing beliefs, but because it is an effective way to uncover lost or hidden information from our memory. Dolores Cannon—a writer, researcher, and hypnotist—was an expert in inducing a somnambulistic state in her subjects for almost fifty years.[4]

Somnambulism, which comes from the French word for "sleepwalker," is a significantly deeper level of relaxation than can be achieved in lighter hypnotic depths, where memories or content can be blocked. Hypnotherapists test for the somnambulistic state by evaluating the subject's responsiveness to specific suggestions. Cannon used this method and past-life regression to obtain hidden information about otherworldly experiences.

Hypnotherapy has proven successful in addressing several psychological and physiological issues, and it is also used to obtain information from subjects about their mental processes. However, it is challenging to verify that hypnosis can be used to retrieve lost or hidden information, and studies on this subject are hard to find. One common and reliable way to test whether the information received is accurate is to ask the subject the same question or to provide a description multiple times over several sessions. If the information remains the same, it can be deemed reliable.

Cannon's work spanned decades, with thousands of subjects providing consistent information on several common themes and topics, such as traumatic events. Early in her career, she began working with people claiming they were abducted by ETs. This quickly evolved to communicating directly with ETs through her hypnosis subjects (we will discuss this in more detail in later chapters). While the consistent reports do not prove the accuracy of the information conveyed by the subjects, they do provide some validation to the fascinating stories and descriptions that her subjects have provided.

Section 1 has laid the groundwork for the awakening process, exploring how we handle change, what we know about the unseen world, and how we form beliefs. Section 2 presents several aspects of our divine connections that will dramatically change how you view yourself and others.

AWAKENING
TO WHO WE
REALLY ARE

SECTION 2

CHAPTER FOUR

WE ARE MULTIDIMENSIONAL BEINGS

"Maybe I'm foolish, maybe I'm blind, but I can see
through this and see what's behind."
—*Rag'n'Bone Man*

Awakening has many layers. In this chapter and the next one, I push you to expand your worldview by showing you that we are living in a three-dimensional box and exploring the dimensions beyond it.

There are two definitions of *dimension*: one relates to measurable characteristics like size and shape, and the other relates to an aspect or feature of something less tangible, like flavor, taste, or smell. This is a great way to explain the dimensions of our reality, which can also be categorized into two distinct groups. The physical model includes the measurable and mathematical characteristics of reality. The spiritual model describes its mental, emotional, and divine characteristics.

When comparing the physical and spiritual models, there is one point of intersection: the third dimension, in which we experience the physical world. In both models, the higher dimensions extend into the unseen world; in the physical model, they are represented by mathematical models, and in the spiritual model, they vibrate beyond our physical senses.

Physical Model

Our physical reality is composed of four dimensions (see Figure 2). Suppose you are on a tennis court playing with a tennis ball with your friend. You roll the ball directly to them in a straight line; that is length, the first dimension. Then your friend rolls the ball back to you, banking it off a wall; that is width, the second dimension. After you start playing a game and hitting the ball over the net, that adds a third dimension: height. The ball can now move the length of the court, move side to side across the court, and change height off the ground. The ball does not move across the court instantaneously; that is the fourth dimension, time. There are caveats to these four dimensions, including the idea that time is flexible.

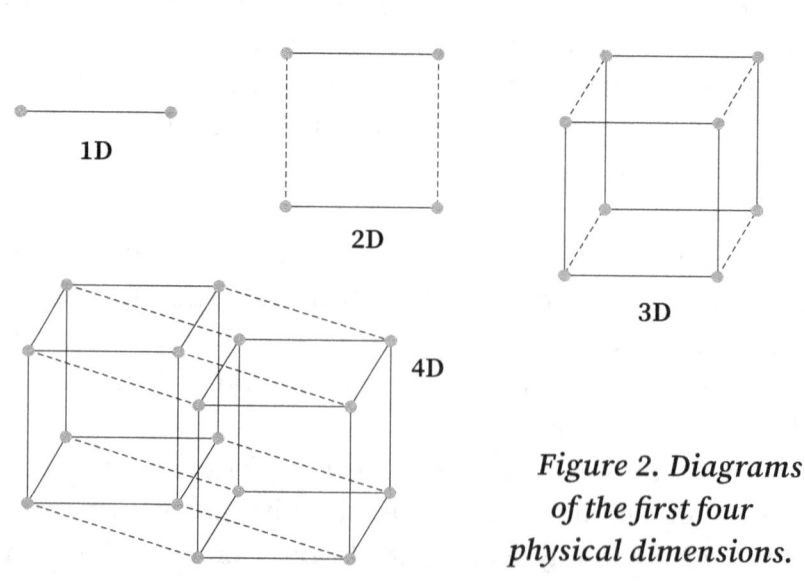

Figure 2. Diagrams of the first four physical dimensions.

HIGHER DIMENSIONS

Beyond the fourth dimension, we leave the observable and measurable for the theoretical models proposed in string theory, initially developed by physicist Gabriele Veneziano, PhD, in 1968, while he was working at the European Organization for Nuclear Research. According to string theory, all the smallest basic particles in the universe are vibrating filaments of energy known as strings. They have no width or height, are much smaller than a proton, and are components of other subatomic particles. The vibrational aspects of these elements may tie in with the vibrations in the Law of Attraction model (see p. 36).

String theory introduces six "curled up" or "compactified" dimensions, so small that they cannot be observed. These are actually mathematical models that outline the characteristics of each of the higher dimensions. Theoretical physicists suggest several possibilities for what these six dimensions look like. For example, they may contain other worlds slightly different than ours, multiple universes, parallel universes, giant membranes, or space-time bubbles. Describing what these higher dimensions look like is like trying to describe the experience of riding a roller coaster by looking at an engineering blueprint of a ride no one knows how to build.

A good example of what the fifth dimension might look like appears in the movie *Interstellar* (2014), directed by Christopher Nolan, which explores wormholes, black holes, and other dimensions as NASA pilot Joseph Cooper (Matthew McConaughey) travels through space to find a new habitable planet for humanity. Toward the end of the movie, advanced beings create a fifth-dimension place for Cooper to communicate with his daughter, Murphy, across time to help her solve a complex gravitational problem. The scene looks

We spend all our
lives in three
dimensions, going
forward and
backward, left
and right, up and
down, thinking that
anything beyond
our pond (our own
little universe) is
science fiction.

something like a fun house of mirrors with repeated images and alternate pathways in multiple directions.

Michio Kaku, PhD, a popular American theoretical physicist, shared a story that illustrates our current dimensional reality. As a child, watching fish swim in a pond, he observed that the fish were living in two dimensions. They had eyes on each side of their head and could swim forward, backward, left, and right, but they could not see him because he was in a third dimension. They did not understand "up" and were unaware of a universe beyond their pond. However, if he had lifted them out of the water, bringing them into the third dimension, they would have seen beings breathing without water and moving without fins—a new reality of biology and physics for them.

Kaku hypothesized that we are like the fish. We spend all our lives in three dimensions, going forward and backward, left and right, up and down, thinking that anything beyond our pond (our own little universe) is science fiction. However, while many of the known laws of physics do not work together in three dimensions, when you go beyond our pond to a hyperspace of more than three dimensions, they all fit together like a jigsaw puzzle. We cannot see beyond our physical world because of our physical limitations, and our minds cannot grasp what other dimensions may look like. However, we can get glimpses of what lies beyond our "box" and interact with beings that reside in other dimensions, or the spiritual world.[1]

Spiritual Model

Western cultures are most familiar with two spiritual dimensions: sleeping states and waking states. (Sometimes, I add a third dimension called "spring break" for college students.) Eastern cultures teach that many more levels of awareness and dimensions exist, although they take years, even lifetimes, of practice to experience.

Where does information about the spiritual dimensions come from? Like all spiritual and religious texts, it comes from humans who have channeled the information. I know what you're probably thinking. People channeling sacred texts from divine sources is one thing, but channeling information from ETs is another. However, I hope that you will try to keep an open mind and suspend your disbelief for a little while to see if any of this chapter rings true for you.

SPIRITUAL DIMENSIONS

The spiritual dimensions were first recognized in the West before World War II and referred to as *planes*. They became popular through the channeled teachings of Edgar Cayce (1877–1945). Over time, the word *dimensions* gradually replaced *planes*, possibly due to the advent of quantum physics and the desire to adopt more scientific terminology.

The spiritual dimension models suggest different numbers of dimensions, from under ten to hundreds, with each dimension having its own characteristics. However, most authors agree that the lower dimensions are dense, heavy, rigid, and narrowly focused on lower-frequency vibrations, with a strong sense of individuality and separation. Higher dimensions are often described as light, transparent, flexible, less complex, and more unified. Their higher-frequency vibrations also hold more knowledge and awareness, as well as an increased sense of universal oneness, accompanied by a decrease in individuality. From a musical perspective, higher dimensions are faster than lower dimensions, just as higher notes on a piano keyboard vibrate at a higher frequency than lower notes.

"There is a reality beyond human reality, beyond human characteristics that you know. And there is knowledge that can never be verbal. And there is experience that cannot be translated in human terms."
—Seth II, channeled through Jane Roberts

In 2023 Alan Lew published "The One Most Complete Guide to the Spiritual Dimensions of Reality,"[2] in which he provided a detailed review of topics related to the spiritual dimensions from several sources, including Seth, a non-physical entity channeled through the American author Jane Roberts from late 1963 until her death in 1984.[3] Lew referenced spiritual thought leaders like the Ra collective, a group of nonphysical entities, and included the teachings of Matías De Stefano, an Argentine philosopher, writer, and media personality.[4] De Stefano is a young and impressive teacher who, from the age of three, could remember and recount many of his past lives, spanning millions of years on a planet in the Sirius star system.

Of the many models of spiritual dimensions available, De Stefano's model, as summarized by Lew, is a good place to start.[5]

First Dimension—Pure Light and Consciousness
Purpose: to be the single pure consciousness of creation; "I Am"

Second Dimension—Polarities and Vibrations (Semi-physical)
Purpose: to create time and space through a diversity of frequencies

Third Dimension—Manifesting Diversity in "Space" (Fully physical)
Purpose: to experience and master our personal diversity of spaces and to manifest separate forms in a fixed time and space

Fourth Dimension—Mastering "Time" (Transitional between physical and nonphysical)
Purpose: to experience and master our personal diversity of timelines and to learn to manipulate time and space

Fifth Dimension—Full Integration of Third and Fourth Dimensions
Purpose: to understand all our third- and fourth-dimension experiences as one (oneness)

Sixth Dimension—Creating Universes and Realities
Purpose: to learn to create entire universes

Seventh Dimension—Enlightenment and Heaven
Purpose: to guide and create all universes and realities

Eighth Dimension—The Akashic Records
Purpose: to be the pure and complete knowledge of creation

Ninth Dimension—The Void Beyond Dimensions
Purpose: to inspire all creation; "I Am All"

Zero Dimension—The Question with No Answer
No purpose or meaning

"Reality is merely an illusion, albeit
a very persistent one."
—*Albert Einstein*

Lew also reviewed some of the principles on which De Stefano's model of reality is based, including De Stefano's argument that dimensions are perspectives, not places where we can go or come from. De Stefano explained that we do not move in a linear path from one dimension to the next; we can temporarily access all dimensions while existing in our physical reality. For example, a person could be meditating in the fifth or seventh dimension while sitting next to someone engrossed in the third dimension, watching a football game on their phone. Finally, according to De Stefano, our goal as beings in the third dimension is to integrate every possible third-dimension experience and perspective, and then to transform consciously from the third dimension to become fourth- and fifth-dimension beings, subsequently experiencing the other dimensions and integrating them into our lives, and ultimately learning that we are gods creating universes and realities.

Dimensions and Densities

One related topic in the discussion of dimensions is densities. These are the vibrational levels experienced within dimensions. It can be confusing because densities have the same titles and characteristics as dimensions, but they are a separate idea from dimensions. Lyssa Royal Holt, through her channeled source Sasha, from the constellation Pleiades, described densities as vibrational levels of consciousness, and dimensions as structural or spatial frameworks. In other words, dimensions are related to a location in space and time, while densities are related to

If you are living in a physical body on Earth, you will always be located in the physical third and fourth dimensions. However, you can experience all the dimensions by shifting your vibrational levels or density. You can increase your density level by expressing gratitude and unconditional love, or engaging in mindfulness, meditation, psychedelic substances, and even in the activities you are engaged in.

levels of awareness that we can tap into at times.[6] Darryl Anka, through his channeled source, Bashar, from the constellation of Orion, explained that densities are like states and dimensions are like countries. Just as you can travel between different states (densities) within the same country (dimension), you can experience different levels of consciousness within the same structural reality. As with dimensions, when we shift from lower vibrational densities to higher ones, we experience less separation from God/Source and others, and experience oneness.[7]

Authors of dimensional models disagree to some extent about whether the fourth dimension is physical, nonphysical, or a transition from physical to nonphysical. However, most agree that, as a species, we are in the process of moving away from the third dimension to the fifth dimension. One way to reconcile this is to imagine we are transitioning from the third to the fifth dimension *through* the fourth dimension. I tend to think that the fourth dimension is physical mainly because we can reach through to the nonphysical world while we are still in the physical third dimension in a variety of ways. We will discuss these in detail in Chapter 6.

We can learn to experience many dimensions while we are physically present in this third dimension by shifting our density. When our resident or long-term density reaches the fifth level, we will transcend from the physical to the nonphysical dimension (see Figure 3).

Dimension	Density	Description
3rd	3rd	Physical
4th	4th	
5th	5th	Non-physical

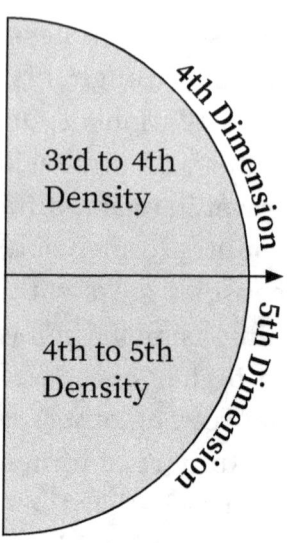

Figure 3. Bashar's dimensions and densities.[8]

To be clear, if you are living in a physical body on Earth, you will always be located in the physical third and fourth dimensions. However, you can experience all the dimensions by shifting your vibrational levels or density. You can increase your density level by expressing gratitude and unconditional love, or engaging in mindfulness, meditation, psychedelic substances, or even what you are focusing your attention on. For example, if you are spending time playing a violent video game or watching a horror movie, you are experiencing the third density. If you are having a romantic dinner or appreciating a beautiful sunset, you are experiencing the fifth density.

As mentioned, many people believe that Earth is transitioning out of the third/fourth dimension to the fifth and fully embracing unity, oneness, and compassion. (I know this can be difficult to accept, especially in 2025. We will discuss this shift in Chapter 7.) Others believe that Earth is moving to the fifth dimension and even splitting into an alternate Earth. This is a much different topic and a discussion for another time.

Understanding that we are living in what we experience as a three-dimensional box and simultaneously existing in other dimensions can be mind-blowing. It is like living in a small but nicely appointed apartment that you are very comfortable in. The kitchen, living room, and dining room are all furnished just right. Then, one day, you open the front door and walk out onto Times Square in New York City. All the lights, cars, trains, sirens, people, buildings, and smells hit you so hard it takes some time to adjust to what is going on and where you are.

The next chapter will provide a way to experience other dimensions for yourself.

CHAPTER FIVE

EXPERIENCING THE SPIRITUAL DIMENSIONS

"The mind is its own place, and in itself can make a
heaven of hell, a hell of heaven."
—*John Milton*

Becoming aware that we are multidimensional beings is crucial in our awakening journey. Once we develop this awareness, we can move in and out of different dimensions, opening up a new world. When I first began researching the spiritual dimensions, I kept coming back to the question, So what? I saw no practical applications or reasons why anyone would want to know about these dimensions. Then I stumbled upon two authors who stood out from all the other sources and put these complex concepts in perspective in a meaningful way.

Authors, astrologers, and publishers Barbara Hand Clow and Gerry Clow became popular in the 1980s and 1990s after publishing several books on astrology and astronomy. Hand Clow was among the first to publish books based on channeled material from an ET—Satya from the Alcyone system in the Pleiades star cluster. I recommend reading Hand Clow's books, specifically *Alchemy of Nine Dimensions: Activating the Full Spectrum of Consciousness* and *The Pleiadian Agenda: A New Cosmology for the Age of Light,* which tells the story of how she initially connected with Satya and learned to understand the information she received.[1]

Hand Clow and Clow's model of the physical and spiritual dimensions differs significantly from the others we have reviewed and, at the same time, is more tangible. Three things stood out to me as I studied Hand Clow and Clow's work. First, Hand Clow was very honest in describing how she began receiving the channeled information and how challenging it was to understand it enough to write about it. Second, because she wanted to verify the information she received with known science as much as possible, she consulted with physicists and mathematicians to unpack the dense, complicated information and compare it with new theories and discoveries in quantum mechanics and mathematical models. Her Cherokee heritage also enabled her to see the deep connections among the Cherokee, Mayan, and Pleiadian descriptions of the dimensions. Third, and most valuable for me, Clow provided commentary to help readers understand what the different dimensions feel like, learn how to navigate through them, and discover how they can impact our lives.

Hand Clow and Clow's model includes the following nine physical and spiritual dimensions.[2]

PHYSICAL DIMENSIONS
First Dimension: The Iron Core Crystal in the Center of Earth

This is the iron core crystal, approximately 1,500 miles in diameter, at the center of our planet. It is the beginning point of all Earth's life forms.

Second Dimension: The Telluric World

This is the outer core and mantle, which contain rocks, magma, and crystals. It is the source of life and heals and energizes the surface.

Third Dimension: Linear Space and Time

This is the dimension of linear space and time in which humans live with all other plants and creatures. Most Indigenous teachers say that in the third dimension, we are mostly asleep. The physical world is held together by frequencies that vibrate to create physical matter. Although appearing solid, it is actually more space than matter.

SEMI-PHYSICAL DIMENSION

Fourth Dimension: The World of Myths and Archetypes

This dimension comprises the human collective mind, the fusion of individual thoughts and feelings that create archetypal patterns connecting all people. It is the first nonphysical dimension we experience and is characterized by separation and polarity.

NONPHYSICAL DIMENSIONS

Fifth Dimension: Samadhi and the Pleiadians

This dimension centers on the human heart. The vibrational frequency is called Samadhi, the human experience of communion with the Divine. It is associated with beings from the Pleiades, who have been the ancestors of many Indigenous peoples on Earth for at least forty thousand years.

Sixth Dimension: Sacred Geometry and Platonia

This is the realm of geometric forms replicating as plants, animals, humans, and material objects in the third dimension, called morphogenesis. Platonia is a term from physics that refers to all possible configurations of the universe.

Seventh Dimension: The Galactic Highways of Light

In this dimension, cosmic sound generates the geometric forms from the sixth dimension by harmonic resonance. In our galaxy, cosmic sound travels within bands of light that are stepped down to lower-frequency seventh-dimension sound waves.

Eighth Dimension: The Divine Mind

The energetic realm of the eighth dimension is why we feel God's love as a constant energy source in our lives.

Ninth Dimension: The Black Hole in the Center of the Milky Way

This dimension projects out of the black hole in the center of the Milky Way galaxy in time waves. These waves attract our attention because we want to understand our origin and seek Spirit in the material world.

A Map of the Dimensions

In Hand Clow's model, we live in the third dimension physically all the time, and consciously in other dimensions some of the time. I say some of the time because we can venture into other dimensions unintentionally through our dreams and near-death experiences, and intentionally through meditation and spiritual therapy sessions.

Our third-dimension life is challenging; some even call it chaotic. It is an intersection of the physical and nonphysical, where we experience linear time and see ourselves as separate from others in a slow-moving, dense world. We are restricted by our verbal and written communication (more highly evolved beings communicate mainly through telepathy). Those who remember what it was like living in the spirit world before incarnating or who can communicate with spiritual beings confirm that there is a drastic difference between living in the third dimension and living in the spiritual realms, where there is lightness, peace, and unity. One downside of the spiritual realms—maybe the only downside—is that those who live there cannot experience the physical world as we do. Beings who have never been incarnated do not know what it's like to swim in the ocean, shop for beautiful clothes, or walk hand in hand with a lover.

In Hand Clow's nine-dimension model, the semi-physical fourth dimension is like a clearinghouse of energy in the form of a canopy between us and the nonphysical higher dimensions (see Figure 4). When higher-frequency energy moves into the fourth-dimension canopy, it acts as a dualistic lens that splits thoughts and feelings into positive or negative, good or evil, black or white, and right or wrong. In the fourth dimension, we are bombarded with stories, dramas, and myths by the television and movie industries; taught about goddesses, angels, demons, and damnation by our religions; and drawn into conflict and war by our politicians. The good news is that we, as a species and a global collective, are moving out of the fourth dimension to adopt a more positive, loving, and unified existence in the fifth dimension.

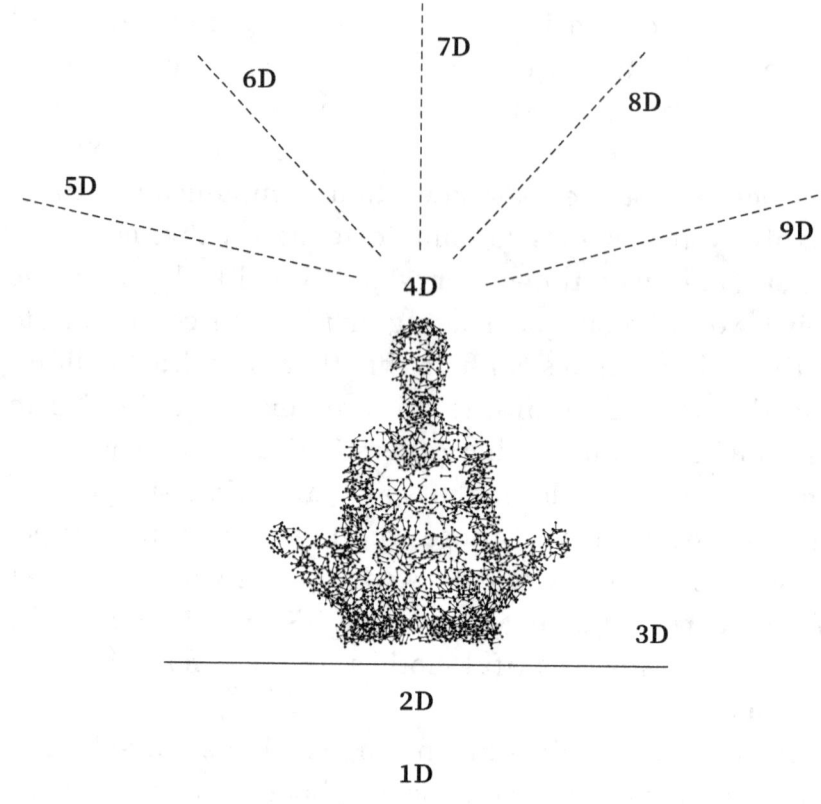

7D

6D

8D

5D

9D

4D

3D

2D

1D

*Figure 4. The lower dimensions (1D and 2D)
serve as grounding dimensions; 3D represents our
physical world; 4D is the canopy that filters all the
higher dimensions; 5D–9D are celestial (adapted from
Alchemy of the Nine Dimensions).*[3]

Experiencing the Dimensions

Some people think that one day, when they are walking down
the street or through a building, they'll pass a ringing phone,
pick it up, and evaporate out of the matrix into another
dimension as in the *Matrix* movie series. It's actually much

easier than that to experience other dimensions, and it is something you can start learning how to do right now.

As a holistic healing practitioner, Clow added a valuable perspective to the nine-dimension model by developing a method to incorporate the dimensions into our lives. He uses variations of craniosacral therapy and energy medicine to essentially help his subjects move through and clear each dimension of any blocks they might have by raising their vibrational frequency through guided meditations or by helping them expand their perspective by talking through the difficulties with them. For example, if you are upset about the conflict in the Middle East and extremely angry about what one side did or said, you are firmly in the fourth dimension. However, you can move away from that feeling by deeply considering both sides of the conflict so that you can understand and empathize with each perspective. By doing this, your vibrational levels rise so that you start experiencing the fifth dimension and begin to feel love and compassion for the people on all sides of the conflict. A big advantage of moving out of the fourth dimension, from my perspective, is that we can move away from uncomfortable feelings of anger and hatred, which have negative effects on both our emotional and our physical health.

Another way to shift to the fifth dimension when dealing with someone who makes you angry is to view them as part of God/Source—no matter who they are or what they have done. Do you see how this might help? You can view the person as an eternal being playing a role in this time and place; in another life, they may be a more loving and compassionate person.

If you have difficulty shifting to the fifth dimension in any situation, do not forget to ask God/Source for help. We

Knowing your orientation
anywhere and anytime
enables you to feel
the energies and spirits
of each direction.
This will help
transform you into
a heart-centered person,
allowing you to attract
what you want and feel a
connection to all things.

often overlook the fact that our spirit team is always near to assist us.

The nine dimensions also correlate with our chakra energy system, and blockages can be addressed—as in chakra balancing—through mindfulness and meditation, yoga and breathing techniques, talk therapy, or creative expression.

Experiential Exercises: Feeling the Dimensions

Now it is time to learn how to experience the nine dimensions. I recommend two techniques: The first is a grounding exercise developed by Hand Clow. It is unique among any other grounding exercises I have used because it has its roots in her Cherokee heritage. The second is Clow's guided meditation.

SEVEN-DIRECTIONAL GROUNDING

This grounding exercise is really more of a lifestyle change than an exercise, although you are encouraged to engage with it daily. If possible, start by identifying a sacred space in your home or office. It can be as simple as the desk you work at, or it can be a separate area with images, figurines, special seating, or incense. As precisely as you can, identify the north, south, east, and west directions in your space. It is useful to place favorite objects, figurines, or pictures in locations that remind you of the directions. These do not need to be obvious to everyone if you share the space; they just need to be obvious to you.

Begin by sitting facing east, with the west to your back, the north to your left, and the south to your right. Knowing where the sun rises and sets will increase your energy and vitality. The fifth direction is straight down into the Earth, and the sixth is straight up to the sky and outer space. The seventh direction is your heart, your center.

Spend time in this space meditating, quieting your mind, or listening to soft music daily or as often as possible, preferably at sunrise or by 11:00 a.m. Fifteen minutes is all you need, but more time is better. Feel in your heart where you are in relation to all the directions; feel that you are grounded.

As you orient your body in the six directions, you will feel yourself as a vibrating, oscillating body and know the following:

- Energies coming to you from the east are spirits who come to offer you creative guidance for the day.

- Energies coming to you from the west are spirits who come to show you what you need to transform and possibly throw away.

- Energies coming to you from the north will inspire you to seek the most challenging outcome of the day.

- Energies coming to you from the south are spirits who want to support and nurture you.

- Energies from the Earth feed you with unlimited powers and strength.

- Energies from the sky connect you to all the higher worlds and higher dimensions.

Knowing your orientation anywhere and anytime enables you to feel the energies and spirits of each direction. This will help transform you into a heart-centered person, allowing you to attract what you want and feel a connection to all things.

GUIDED MEDITATION

Clow's therapeutic sessions correlate the nine dimensions to our chakra energy system. While it is always ideal to conduct therapeutic sessions in person, he graciously offers recordings of his guided meditations for each of the nine dimensions and related chakras. In addition, Michael Stearns, an American musician and composer, created an album, *Journey through Nine Dimensions*, to help us experience each dimension.

Since it was not feasible for me to travel to Santa Fe, New Mexico, for a live session with Clow, I downloaded the guided meditation and musical files and listened to the musical soundtrack for each dimension at least once, and then to the corresponding guided meditation. Following each meditation, I played the corresponding soundtrack throughout the day.

This has had a profound impact on my life, and I encourage you to listen to these recordings in whatever way feels comfortable to you. Listening to the meditations, you will be better able to feel

- The first dimension at the coccygeal or root;

- The second dimension at the sacral or sexual chakra;

- The third dimension at both your root and also sexual chakras;

- The fourth dimension at the solar plexus chakra;

- The fifth dimension at the heart chakra;

- The sixth dimension at the throat chakra;

- The seventh dimension at the third eye chakra;

- The eighth dimension at the crown chakra; and

- The ninth dimension at the crown chakra.

Stearns's album and Clow's guided meditations are available for free digital download when you purchase Hand Clow and Clow's book *Alchemy of Nine Dimensions* (twentieth anniversary edition).

CHAPTER SIX

PIERCING THE VEIL

"To pierce the veil is to transcend the illusion of separation, to see that the physical and spiritual are but two sides of the same divine coin."
—*Eckhart Tolle*

We tend to perceive our lives as embedded in physicality, duality, and separateness. With some effort, we can connect with the Divine and the unseen world, supercharging our experiences of love, compassion, and unity. However, to have a relationship with the spirit world, we need to be able to step beyond our baseline reality through what is called "the veil."

There are many definitions of *veil*, from a simple piece of cloth to symbolic functions in religious and cultural traditions. In the context of this book, the veil is the barrier separating the physical world from the spiritual. In dimensional terms, this does not mean moving from the third-dimension physical world to the nonphysical dimensions because we can experience all dimensions while being in our physical bodies. Instead, it means that while we are here, we can transcend beyond the confines of our bodies into the nonphysical and spiritual realms,

"You think you
know how the
world works?
What if I told you
that reality is
one of many?"

—Doctor Strange *(2016)*

where we can interact with spirits, ancestors, and other unseen entities. Interestingly, the veil's transparency changes globally when it becomes "thin" at certain times of the year—for example, around Halloween—providing easier access to the spirit world.

> "You think you know how the world works?
> What if I told you that reality is one of many?"
> —Doctor Strange *(2016)*

I believe there are six common ways to transcend or pierce the veil.

- **Natural Sensitivity**—Many people, at a very early age, have a connection with the spirit world. They may have memories of other lives or remember preparing to come to Earth, or they may have had relationships with angels, passed loved ones, or other beings for as long as they can remember.

- **Trauma**—People who experience trauma can develop an increased sensitivity to and have interactions with the spirit world. This may be a coping mechanism, or the spirit world may step up its involvement to help them through these extremely hard times.

- **Study**—Some people, like me, develop their natural spiritual or psychic abilities or sensitivities through reading; working with mediums, psychic teachers, and mentors; or classes. A few years ago, if someone had asked me if I was psychic or a medium, I would have told them, "Absolutely not." However, after only a few years of dedicated work, guidance from friends, and support from my spirit team, I have become very active on both fronts.

- **Meditative States**—Calming the mind is a critical step in spiritual growth and the awakening process. Through meditation, we can become more aware of our thoughts and emotions, experience profound connections with the Divine, and transcend our third-dimension reality. Numerous books, apps, classes, and workshops on meditation are available for students of all levels, many at no cost.

- **Near-Death Experiences (NDEs)**—Raymond Moody, MD, introduced the term "near-death experience" in 1975 in his book *Life after Life*.[1] An NDE is a subjective experience that people report after being clinically dead, near death, or in a situation where death is likely or expected. Experiences during these times range from relatively simple to intense spiritual encounters.

- **Psychedelic Drugs**—There is ample evidence that substances like lysergic acid diethylamide (LSD), psilocybin, and dimethyltryptamine (DMT) can produce profound mystical experiences characterized by feelings of unity, transcendence, and interconnectedness with all things.

We will focus on these last two topics for the remainder of the chapter.

Near-Death Experiences

People who have had NDEs can provide detailed information about what it is like beyond the veil and show us a world beyond our wildest dreams. There have been thousands of reports of NDEs collected throughout history from around the world. In Moody's seminal book *Life after Life*, he shared the results of 150 interviews with people describing NDEs. They identified common elements, such as out-of-body experiences, feelings of peace, a tunnel experience, seeing beings and bright lights, and a life review.

In 2009, thirty years after Moody's initial work, three NDE researchers—Janice Miner Holden, EdD; Bruce Greyson, MD; and Debbie James, MSN, RN—published *The Handbook of Near-Death Experiences*.[2] They reviewed the NDE research from 1975 to 2005, identifying 55 research teams, 65 published studies, and 700 journal articles involving 3,500 NDEs. Their research confirmed and refined Moody's work but did not uncover any contradictory information.

Holden, Greyson, and James's research found that the vast majority of NDEs were pleasurable; those study participants who described the experiences as unpleasant did so not necessarily because they were painful, but because the participants did not like the out-of-body experience or feeling out of control. One of the most dramatic positive experiences reported was the feeling of tremendous peace, well-being, safety, and ecstasy. One person described the feeling of experiencing all their favorite things in life—amplified by a million. In addition, the study participants noted that when their consciousness left their body, all their associated bodily pain dissipated immediately. Many also said that their experiences seemed more "real" than the life they had just left; colors were indescribably more colorful and clear, as were other sights and sounds. Some subjects explained that they could see through walls to other rooms or through the back of their own body. Others reported that they were able to travel to places just by thinking about a location or person. This is not surprising, given that when we interact with deceased loved ones or spiritual beings, our communication occurs not through words but through

"It is not the end of
the physical body
that should worry us.
Rather, our concern
must be to live while
we're alive."

—*Elisabeth Kübler-Ross*

thoughts; language was designed for communication in the third-dimension reality.

Skeptics of NDEs usually claim that the reported stories and visions are the result of auditory and visual hallucinations caused by a lack of oxygen, decreased blood flow to the brain, or the brain shutting down. While this explanation has some merit for understanding a few of the experiences, Holden maintained that these physiological states do not explain every aspect of NDEs.

"It is not the end of the physical body that should worry us.
Rather, our concern must be to live while we're alive."
—*Elisabeth Kübler-Ross*

Some reports of NDEs allow us to verify that these experiences are real. For example, in his book *Light and Death*, Dr. Michael Sabom presented the case of Pam Reynolds. During a surgical procedure, her heartbeat, breathing, and brain activity stopped and she had an NDE. After she regained consciousness, she provided a detailed description of the surgery, which was verified as accurate.

The Handbook of Near-Death Experiences includes the story of a patient who had an NDE after going into cardiac arrest while in surgery. During his NDE, the patient could hear the surgeon's thoughts about a minor car accident he had been in on the way to the hospital and was aware of the surgeon's preoccupation with the accident and how it would work out with his insurance. The patient recovered and, to his surgeon's surprise, told him, "Don't worry. Everything is going to work out with the insurance."

It is important to note that the available research does not reveal any differences in the occurrences or characteristics of NDEs with regard to age, gender, ethnicity, religious beliefs, or the nature of the person experiencing them. Holden stressed that in the thousands of NDEs she studied, only one person reported having a judgmental experience; all the other NDEs were characterized as positive, accepting, and safe.

NDEs provide a glimpse into the world beyond our third-dimension experience, and many people report that an NDE has profoundly changed their lives. The following are the most common experiences during an NDE.

- **Out-of-Body Experience**: Many people report feeling as though they are floating above their physical body and observing the scene around them.

- **Peace and Painlessness**: Those who have experienced an NDE often describe a profound sense of peace and the absence of pain.

- **Rapid Movement through Darkness**: Some individuals describe moving through a dark tunnel or void at high speed.

- **Encounter with a Light**: A bright, indescribable light is often reported, which can be accompanied by feelings of love and warmth.

- **Encounter with Beings of Light**: People often report meeting deceased loved ones, religious figures, or other beings of light.

- **Life Review**: Many people experience a review of their life, reliving events and experiencing the emotional impact of their actions on others.

- **Sense of Being Somewhere Else**: A feeling of being in a different realm or spiritual world is often reported.

- **Rapid Thought Processes**: Sharp, clear thinking and observations are common.

- **Reluctance to Return**: Many people express a reluctance to come back to their physical bodies.

- **Distorted Sense of Time and Space**: Time and space may seem irrelevant or nonexistent.

Experiential Exercise

Scott M. Taylor, EdD, has been an NDE researcher and author for more than thirty years. Based on his analysis of more than six thousand NDE case studies, he developed a guided meditation series incorporating a consciousness-expanding technology (Hemi-Sync®). This approach uses binaural beats to help individuals achieve the altered states of consciousness frequented by those who have had NDEs. I bought the digital recording of Taylor's NDE meditation *Into the Light: Meet Your Guides* and had a very meaningful session connecting with God/Source.[3] I felt transported to a room where I met two of my spirit guides and finally got their names, which I had been asking to receive for some time. I discovered that once you go through this meditation, you can quickly return to the place it transports you as often as you would like.

Psychedelic Drugs

When compared to the other ways to pierce the veil, psychedelics can propel us into other dimensions quickly, while providing intense and profound experiences. Many people associate psychedelic drugs with the counterculture movement of the 1960s in the United States and Europe, which popularized the use of LSD and psilocybin. However, these substances have been used as sacraments in religious rituals, ceremonies, and healing practices for thousands of years. Today scientific research focuses on the potential of psychedelics to impact profound spiritual experiences, enhance personal growth, and address addiction and other psychological disorders.

The most popular psychedelics are psilocybin, ayahuasca, LSD, DMT, and ibogaine:

- **Psilocybin**: Also known as "magic mushrooms," psilocybin can elicit mystical-type experiences, with feelings of unity, interconnectedness, and transcendence. Psilocybin-assisted therapy is also used in clinical settings for treating depression, anxiety, and existential distress while fostering spiritual insights and personal growth.

- **Ayahuasca**: Frequently used in Amazonian shamanic ceremonies, ayahuasca contains a combination of psychoactive compounds, including DMT and monoamine oxidase inhibitors (MAOIs). Participants in ceremonies like these often report deeply spiritual experiences involving purging, introspection, and connection with nature and the Divine. Ayahuasca has been associated with intense healing and spiritual experiences.

- **LSD**: LSD is an ergot-derived synthetic psychedelic compound known for its powerful effects on consciousness and experiences of ego dissolution, interconnectedness, and spiritual awakening. LSD-assisted therapy has shown some efficacy in treating conditions such as PTSD and addiction.

- **DMT:** A naturally occurring compound found in plants, animals, and even the human brain, DMT is known for eliciting intense visual and auditory hallucinations, often described as breakthrough experiences or encounters with otherworldly entities. DMT-containing substances like ayahuasca and smoked DMT have been used in traditional and contemporary contexts for spiritual exploration and healing.

- **Ibogaine:** Derived from the root bark of the West African iboga plant, ibogaine is used as a treatment for addiction and for facilitating profound introspection and spiritual insights. Ibogaine ceremonies, often conducted through guided sessions, can lead to deep psychological exploration, emotional healing, and spiritual awakening.

Research suggests that psychedelic drugs, when used in supportive settings, can stimulate profound mystical experiences characterized by unity, transcendence, and positive emotions, with some studies reporting long-term effects. For example, one study examining the effects of psilocybin in thirty-five participants who had never used psychedelic drugs found that about 60 percent of participants reported experiences such as unity with all things, transcendence of time and space, a sense of insight into the ultimate nature of reality, and feelings of ineffability, awe, and other profound positive emotions such as joy, peace, and love. At a fourteen-month follow-up, more than half of the participants rated the psilocybin-occasioned experience as among the five most personally meaningful and spiritually significant experiences of their life.[4]

It's important to note that people who use psychedelics tend to embrace mystical beliefs and place greater value on spirituality compared to users of other illegal drugs or those who do not use drugs. This means that it is unclear whether the use of psychedelics induces these beliefs or individuals with preexisting spiritual tendencies are more likely to use these drugs to achieve the results they expect. The potential therapeutic benefits of psychedelics include increased well-being, life satisfaction, and altruism, but these drugs do not necessarily improve users' ability to cope with stress.

AN AYAHUASCA ENGAGEMENT

A friend of mine shared an interesting story about the value of psychedelic drug use. He and his girlfriend occasionally experimented with psychedelics. When he was ready to propose to her, he bought an engagement ring and hid it in his house, waiting for the right moment. One weekend, shortly after he purchased the ring, he and his girlfriend decided to take ayahuasca, a powerful psychedelic. They planned to take turns with the drug so that one could monitor the other while they experienced their trip. While taking ayahuasca, my friend had a profound experience; he had the feelings of bliss, unity, and connectedness that he was accustomed to, in addition to an out-of-body experience, but something else also happened. He was approached by a group of beings, possibly angels, who offered him a choice: he could come with them into the spirit world to start a new life or return to his body and the physical world. He understood that if he chose to go with them, he would die that night. This was not really a choice for him; he loved his girlfriend and could not imagine being without her. However, he was unsure if the decision was entirely up to him. He feared that the beings might take him before he could propose to his girlfriend and let her know how much he loved her. So, even though he was still under the influence of the powerful drug, he decided to get the ring and propose to her. Barely able to walk, he crawled to the room where the ring was hidden, intermittently collapsing to the floor. His girlfriend was concerned and repeatedly asked him what was wrong, but he could hardly speak. He finally retrieved the ring and, in barely intelligible English, asked her to marry him. She immediately said, "Yes," thus cementing a most exciting engagement story.

EXPERIENTIAL ACTIVITY

Look for psychedelic communities or groups where you live. Many have regular meetings combining lectures and experiential sessions. The advantage of these groups is that the presenters usually have strong backgrounds using particular drugs and can offer guidance in experiential sessions. Many are clinicians and therapists who use psychedelics with their patients.

NOTE: Do not attempt to use psychedelic drugs alone or with others who do not have experience using them. Check with your medical doctor and/or behavioral health provider before experimenting with these drugs.

CHAPTER SEVEN

A GLOBAL SHIFT

"The universe is not outside of you. Look inside yourself;
everything that you want, you already are."
—*Rumi*

Most of us wake up slowly. The sun may gradually light up our bedroom, the dog may bark to go outside, or we may snooze our alarm half a dozen times, delaying the inevitable. For many, spiritual awakening is just as gradual. That's how it happened to me; my awakening happened slowly and evolved over decades. I began by clinging to the faith I was born into. When my life fell apart despite my beliefs, I connected directly with God/Source and never looked back.

Over the centuries, humankind has been on a positive evolutionary path. Significant strides in medical care, technology, social and ethical issues, and education have propelled us forward—despite some setbacks. A series of Protestant movements centered on personal religious experiences began in the American colonies and parts of Europe in the mid-1700s and lasted into the 1900s, marking this period as the Great Awakening. However, the impact of the Great Awakening has been waning in recent decades, making way for another awakening. The shift occurring now—from organized religion to spiritual beliefs—will take us to a place humans have never been before.

Numerous surveys and census reports in the United States and around the world indicate that an increasing number of people are not affiliated with a religion, identifying as spiritual rather than religious, adopting New Age beliefs, and seeking psychic services. There are a few possible reasons for this shift, including the publicized scandals within religious groups, our ability to investigate and connect with spiritual communities online, the rise of individuality, and the desire to connect with the Divine and spiritual world directly.

A study conducted by the Pew Research Center in 2023 confirmed the trend of people becoming more spiritual than religious. The study asked participants about their religious and spiritual beliefs—not just in the moment, but also "over the course of their lifetime." Figure 5 summarizes the responses.[1]

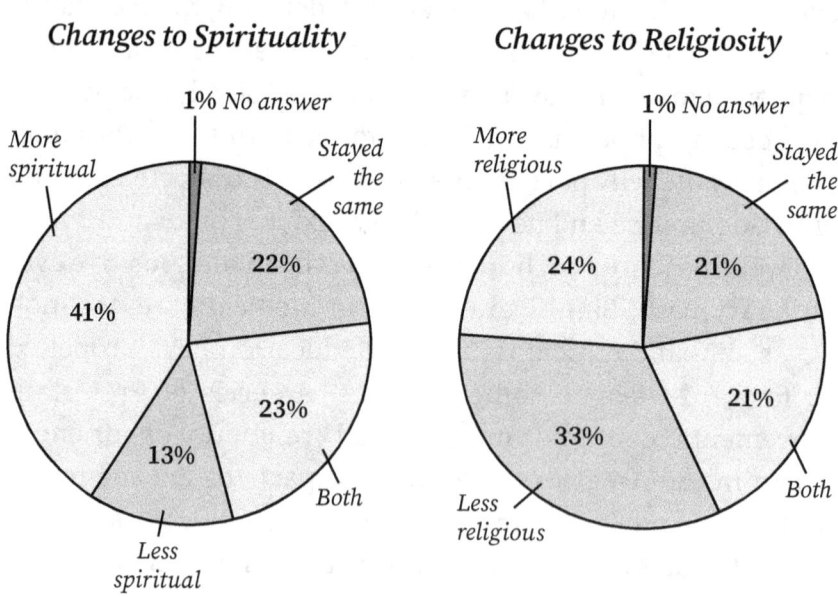

Figure 5. A summary of the results of a 2023 Pew Research Center study on changes to Americans' spirituality and religiosity over the course of their lifetime.

In addition, the study results showed the following:

- Eighty-three percent of the survey participants believe people have a soul or spirit in addition to a physical body.

- Eighty-one percent believe there is something spiritual beyond the natural world, even if we cannot see it.

- Seventy-four percent believe there are some things that science cannot possibly explain.

- Forty-five percent have had a sudden feeling of connection with something from beyond this world.

- Thirty-eight percent have had a strong feeling that someone who has passed away was communicating with them from beyond this world.

- Thirty percent have personally encountered a spirit or unseen spiritual force.

Meditation

One key factor influencing the growing awakening is meditation. Hundreds of studies investigating the effects of meditation on individuals have been conducted. In my doctoral dissertation, "The Effects of Prayer and Meditation on the Quality of Life in Older Adults" (The Fielding Graduate University, 2005), I reviewed the research on the impact of meditation on physical and emotional health. Group meditation can lead to psychological and physiological benefits, such as reduced stress, improved mental health, and enhanced overall well-being.

"You need to learn how to select your thoughts just the same way you select your clothes every day. This is a power you can cultivate."

—*Elizabeth Gilbert*

"You need to learn how to select your thoughts just the same way you select your clothes every day. This is a power you can cultivate."
— *Elizabeth Gilbert*

The number of people meditating is increasing. For example, as of 2022, 17.3 percent of adults in the United States practiced meditation, a significant increase from 7.5 percent in 2002.[2] Worldwide, an estimated two to five hundred million adults meditate. With 7.9 billion people in the world, approximately 5.89 billion (74.5 percent) aged 15 and over, this means that approximately 3.4–8.5 percent of the global population currently meditates.[3]

The growing number of people meditating may have two potential impacts on our planet. First, it will likely increase global vibrational levels, which will, in turn, lead to widespread cooperation, kindness, and unity—a global awakening. Second, according to an article by Neil Wakeling, who has degrees in electronic engineering and music technology, the electronic frequencies of the Earth, known as the Schumann resonances, are changing.[4]

The Schumann resonances can be described as the planet's electric heartbeat. Historically, the planet has emitted base frequencies of 7.83 Hz, with spikes called harmonics. In recent years, these spikes have risen to approximately 14.3 Hz to 20.8 Hz, and on April 24, 2020, the harmonics registered as high as 156 Hz.[5] The human brain operates across several frequencies that coincide with the Schumann resonances. Has the increased number of people meditating across the globe impacted the electromagnetic frequencies of the planet? If so, can changes in the Schumann resonances impact how the human brain works? We don't yet know.

Astrological Landscape

The evidence for our spiritual awakening comes from many sources. One source is astrology, which has been around for thousands of years. Ancient civilizations in Mesopotamia, Egypt, and Greece tracked celestial movements, recording them in cave markings and writings along with their associated meanings and predictions. While there is no scientific validation that astrological transits (planetary positions in the sky) impact our lives, it is interesting to note that common themes occur when specific alignments appear. In particular, the movements of two planets have caught my eye regarding awakening and spiritual growth.

PLUTO

In March 2023, Pluto entered Aquarius, meaning that, as seen from Earth, Pluto is moving through the sky in association with the constellation Aquarius. This alignment occurs approximately every 250 years and will last for the next 20 years. Most astrologers agree that this can be a time of revolutionary change, a time for breaking away from old patterns and embracing new ways of thinking. This could take the form of wholesale transformations and disruptions of societal systems, including technology and collective thinking, leading to a shamanistic transformation (interacting with the spirit world).

Interestingly, when this alignment occurred in the past, it coincided with the Protestant Reformation, the Roman Inquisition, the publication of Nicolaus Copernicus's book on the sun-centered solar system, the discovery of the vaccine for smallpox, the American Revolution, and the French Revolution, among other significant events and innovations.

Regarding the next twenty years, astrologer Torrence Tremayne suggested, "We can surmise the profound

Plutonian metamorphosis of our cosmological perspective of the universe and our place in it as human beings. Potential revelations related to consciousness, extraterrestrials, time-space, the fabric of reality itself."[6]

SATURN

In March 2025, Saturn entered Pisces. While this alignment will last for just 11 months, until February 2026, it only occurs every 29.5 years and can be intense. This planet and constellation are opposites in nature, with Saturn being the workhorse planet—representing structure, discipline, and limitations—and Pisces being sensitive, compassionate, intuitive, and creative. As a result, this alignment will cause increased seriousness about spirituality, mysticism, and metaphysics, and challenge the status quo. Historical events that occurred during this alignment when it arose in the past include the 1997 Asian financial crisis, Princess Diana's passing, the dot-com financial boom, Hong Kong's return to China, and the launch of the internet.

Solar Cycles

The small, recurring variations in Earth's rotation may also be influencing the growing spiritual awakening. The Earth wobbles on its axis like a top that is slowing down, and this plays a key role in influencing Earth's climate over tens of thousands to hundreds of thousands of years. Climate scientists believe that the Milankovitch cycles, which describe the effects of the changes in Earth's movements over thousands of years, influence changes in climate over time.[7] Some spiritual traditions believe they also have a metaphysical effect on the human population. The Milankovitch cycles have three key features: eccentricity, obliquity, and precession.

In 2011–12 we moved into the spring cycle of consciousness, causing our deep sense of separation, aloneness, and polarity to begin shifting into a more integrated reality. This blossoming will continue for the next thirteen thousand years.

- **Eccentricity**: The shape of Earth's orbit around the sun changes over about one hundred thousand years. This corresponds to significant shifts in the collective consciousness of humanity, enlightenment, and spiritual awakening.

- **Obliquity**: The angle of Earth's axial tilt changes over about forty-one thousand years. This cycle influences the alignment of Earth's chakras and brings about periods of spiritual growth and transformation.

- **Precession**: Earth's rotational axis wobbles over a period of approximately twenty-six thousand years. Interestingly, this period matches the time it takes Earth's axis to complete one full cycle of the zodiac. Precession marks the transition between different ages, such as the Age of Pisces and the Age of Aquarius. The movement through the zodiac is associated with the evolution of human consciousness and spiritual awakening. Scientists state that we are at a midpoint in the current precession.

Hinduism follows Earth's precessional cycles and divides them into four time periods—called yugas—totaling 25,290 years. Each of the yugas—Satya, Treta, Dwapara, and Kali—represents a specific phase of humanity's spiritual evolution. Although there are conflicting interpretations of the exact timing of the phases, many Hindus believe we are coming to the end of the Kali yuga cycle. A decline in virtues—such as increased dishonesty and materialism—and a decrease in family values and respect for elders characterizes this cycle. We are beginning the Satya yuga, often called the Golden Age, which is characterized by significant transformations in truth, virtue, and harmony in society and individually.[8]

Lyssa Royal Holt, an educator, channeler, and author since 1985, focuses on understanding consciousness and awareness beyond human identity. For the last thirty years, she has channeled Sasha, a Pleiadian female. In a live event that created the content for Mike Dooley's book *The Great Awakening*, Sasha spoke through Holt and explained that Earth's precession is like our seasons. In the winter, many plants go dormant, and in the spring, they start to bloom. During the last thirteen thousand years, Earth has been experiencing a deep autumn and winter cycle. Sasha said, "In this type of cycle, you have the sense of being in a much more separated and dormant state of consciousness growth." She explained that in 2011–12 we moved into the spring cycle of consciousness, causing our deep sense of separation, aloneness, and polarity to begin shifting into a more integrated reality. This blossoming will continue for the next thirteen thousand years.[9]

Thus, although it might seem like we are entering a period devoid of any spiritual direction, structure, or definition, this is not the case. Many people foresee a new world order on the rise.

THE GREAT PURIFICATION

The Hopi people of North America have predicted a coming period known as the "Great Purification." This prophecy describes a time of extreme upheaval in several aspects of society that precedes a new world. The final sign is the appearance of the Blue Star Kachina, or Saquasohuh, which signifies the beginning of a new world. This sign will appear as a blue star, marking the "Day of Purification," and precedes a worldwide cataclysm that destroys the current world and heralds the birth of a new one.[10]

A New Earth

The idea of evolving to create a better version of ourselves, which many call the "New Earth," may first have been discussed in the sacred texts of Christianity and Islam. Revelation 21:1–4 from the Christian Bible reads, "Then I saw a new heaven and a new earth, for the first heaven and the first earth had passed away." Surah Ibrahim 48 (14:48) from the Quran states, "On the Day when the earth will be changed to a different earth, and so will be the heavens, and they [i.e., all creatures] will come out before Allah, the One, the Prevailing."

The contemporary books that use the term "New Earth" in the title are all science fiction novels, except for one written by Eckhart Tolle, published in 2005, *A New Earth: Awakening to Your Life's Purpose*. In this book, Tolle explained that the New Earth is not a physical place that we will arrive at someday, but rather a new consciousness that is emerging within each one of us. He mapped out how humans can evolve to higher consciousness by breaking free from the trappings of ego and embracing our true eternal self. This requires a shift in vibration, a transition from the Old Earth's dense third-dimension consciousness of separation to the lighter, higher frequency of fifth-dimension consciousness.[11]

In his *A New Earth* audiobook, Tolle explained that the New Earth will take form as we experience an internal transformation of human consciousness through an understanding of our divine nature and connection to all life. Tolle and Neale Donald Walsch discussed this transformation, which will happen gradually and inconsistently for most of us. Tolle encouraged listeners not to be discouraged by the process of this awakening but instead to concentrate on their intentions to change. Walsch also predicted that this transition would not be easy and that we would go through a storm before the calm.

Also in the audiobook, Tolle spoke with Dr. Lothar Schäfer, professor emeritus at the University of Arkansas and a renowned quantum chemist, about the idea of natural evolution on this planet. Dr. Schäfer explained that evolution occurs in jumps, usually following times of distress. Out of this distress, a new version of humans emerges based on cooperation, not competition; kindness and support, not violence and war. Both authors agreed that it is an optimistic perspective, but not an unrealistic one.

Tolle referred to this shift in perspective as unity consciousness, which is characterized by love, acceptance, and unity between humans and God/Source. Unity consciousness is discussed in detail in Chapters 9 and 10.

The Library

Another source of information about the coming awakening is Dolores Cannon's book *The Guardians*. Drawing on fifty years of work with thousands of subjects using deep hypnotic, somnambulistic states, she described a common theme that emerged, which many of her subjects called "The Library." Cannon explained that although her approach unlocked memories of her subjects' current lives, past lives, and interactions with ETs, she believed that the best information came when they were taken to the in-between-lives state. In this state, we are freed from the limitations of a particular body or identity and have access to a place in the spirit realm with no limits to knowledge. Cannon's subjects described what the library looks like: some said it appears as a typical earthly building with shelves of books, and others conveyed that information is displayed on walls in holographic three-dimensional images. Cannon surmised that the visual form of the library is adjusted to the perceptions of the individual. In Cannon's experience, a caretaker or guardian often greeted her and the subject as they entered.[12]

During one session, Cannon and her subject were discussing Earth's history and evolutionary path when a librarian spoke directly to them:

> It is important for you to know that after the upcoming period of turmoil and the Earth changes, there will be much smooth sailing. There will be much learning. There will be assistance involving interplanetary travel. You will begin to know more about your universe and all of the many others. There will be assistance from those in other space realms, and you will join in with that. There will be a communion, *a knowledgeable,* on both sides, working-together. You have not had that before. Other entities in space have known about you, but you have not known about them. And that will happen. There will be smooth sailing. Quite a relief after the turmoil that has been taking place.[13]

Both quantitative and qualitative sources indicate that a large-scale shift in how we view ourselves in relation to the Divine is taking place. This is not an insignificant change, and as we start to grasp that God/Source is not "out there" but part of us—and an extension of the Divine—we will understand Who we really are. In order to do this, we must understand that we are all connected, as we will discuss in the coming chapters.

CHAPTER EIGHT

THE SCIENCE OF CONSCIOUSNESS

"All points in time and space are connected."
—Albert Einstein

I magine eating an apple. First, the rods and cones in the retina of your eye convert the image of the apple into electronic signals. These signals are sent via the optic nerve to the back of your brain, specifically to the visual cortex, where they are interpreted and then matched with your memory. You recognize this object as an apple. As you bite into the apple, your taste buds and olfactory system also confirm that you are ingesting an apple. Collectively, the physical inputs and your memory create the conscious experience of eating an apple.

The Easy and Hard Problems of Consciousness

A cognitive scientist and prominent thought leader on the subject of consciousness, David J. Chalmers, PhD, explained that there are many problems when studying consciousness because it is an ambiguous term with many associated phenomena that impact our sense of reality. In approaching

The physical
sensory inputs of
eating an apple
are one thing, but
the experience of
eating an apple is
something beyond
the physical senses.

the subject, Chalmers divided these problems into two categories: "hard" and "easy."[1]

The easy problems are related to the neural processes we know very well. In the example of eating the apple, the physical receptors, the nervous system, and different parts of the brain piece together what is happening. These inputs and processes can, for the most part, be explained scientifically. Chalmers stated, "Although we do not yet have anything close to a complete explanation of these phenomena, we have a clear idea of how we might go about explaining them."[2]

The hard problems that arise when studying consciousness are related to understanding the experience of our reality. Chalmers cited Thomas Nagel, who studied what lies beyond physical inputs and bodily sensations. Nagel explained that one way to describe consciousness is to identify that there is "something it is like," meaning that, in our example of the apple, all the physical sensory inputs of eating an apple are one thing, but the experience of eating an apple is something beyond the physical senses.[3] In other words, we know what it is like to eat an apple not because our body and mind have registered and interpreted the information, but only because we have eaten one.

Let's look at another example: if you want to understand the experience of sky diving, you can research parachuting and learn that your plane will take off and ascend to 10,500 feet and then you will jump out of the plane strapped to the guy with the chute and free-fall for about thirty seconds. He will pull the cord, and you'll float down to a soft landing. However, you will only really know what it is like to sky dive when you are sitting at the door of your plane, looking two miles down to the ground, and knowing that is where you are about to go—without a plane. Believe me.

Two Concepts Tested

In April 2025, the results of a seven-year study exploring the origins of consciousness were published in the prestigious scientific journal *Nature*.[4] The data came from a consortium of forty-one neuroscientists, neurologists, psychiatrists, and psychologists from prominent academic institutions around the world. The authors tracked blood flow and measured the electrical activity and magnetic fields of over 250 subjects to determine how the brain might process consciousness. The study explored two models of the origin of consciousness: first, the idea that our experience of consciousness arises from a unifying process of the sensations generated from our physical senses (integrated information theory); and second, the traditional belief that consciousness originates from cognitive processes, such as thinking and reasoning (global neuronal workspace theory). While the study had mixed results and did not indicate a clear "winner" between the two models, it did demonstrate that consciousness seems to depend more on sensory processing than previously thought—meaning, our physical experience of the world might be more central to consciousness than was once believed—and hints that the sensation of consciousness may be separate from the brain.[5]

OUR BRAINS AS FILTERS?

A related idea shared by a few researchers is that our brains and nervous systems are designed to be filters. By restricting all the other frequencies of energy that surround us, we can experience the physical world in a focused and uniform manner. This aligns with the idea that, for whatever reason, we exist in the third dimension which is time-bound, dense, and in an environment of separation. The reason why we are here is to learn, through this limited setting, things no being can know or understand if they were never incarnated here. And, from what I have learned, many ETs are envious of the many physical experiences we have on a daily basis.

Could the nonphysical component of consciousness that scientists have begun to identify be the mind or soul that exists beyond our bodies? Here is an example that might shed some light on this question. Suppose you are trying to quiet your mind in meditation or you need to concentrate on a task. As you try to focus, thoughts about what you have to do that day or some issue that needs to be resolved keep popping up and distracting you. This means that a part of your mind is trying to do one thing, while other parts of your mind are generating disruptive thoughts. Who or what is noticing that these thoughts are distracting you? Who or what is observing your thoughts? One answer is that it is the nonphysical consciousness. Whatever it is, it is beyond our current understanding and the scope of empirical research, yet it is nonetheless an integral part of Who we are.

Consciousness and the Soul

From a scientific perspective, consciousness is the awareness of inputs and memories that may or may not be bound by the physical body. In this book, when we discuss the nonphysical aspect of consciousness, it is the seat of our soul. Part of the awakening process is understanding that our consciousness and intentions can interact with our physical world in many ways, also known as mind-matter interaction.

MIND-MATTER INTERACTION

Empirical research has long confirmed that our mental intentions can influence the physical world. Extensive studies on tossed dice and random number generators (RNGs) demonstrate this mind-matter interaction.

Research on tossed dice has been conducted for decades, with a focus on whether participants are able to mentally influence dice so that a specific face number appears face up when they are tossed. The studies hypothesized that participants would be able to influence the dice to show a specific number (called a hit). While the results of many tossed-dice studies show only a slight percentage difference from chance (1.2 percent), these results are statistically significant, meaning that they verify that the participants' mental intentions changed how the dice behaved.

Studies using RNGs can be viewed as an electronic counterpart to dice studies, and hundreds have been conducted. These studies test participants' ability to mentally influence a circuit that produces a stream of approximately one thousand random ones or zeroes per second. This means that the chance of the circuit producing either a one or a zero is 50 percent. Dean Radin, known for his extensive research in parapsychology—focusing on phenomena such as telepathy, precognition, and psychokines—analyzed more than eight hundred RNG studies. He discovered a small but statistically significant change from chance, meaning that participants were able to change the outcomes of the RNG through their mental intentions. Radin concluded his review of mind-matter interaction by stating:

> After 60 years of experiments using tossed dice and their modern progeny, electronic RNGs, researchers have produced persuasive, consistent replicated evidence that mental intention is associated with the behavior of these physical systems. We know that the experimental results are not due to chance, selected reporting, poor

experimental design, only a few individuals, or only a few experimenters.[6]

There are many other examples of how our conscious intentions can impact the physical world. Dr. Masaru Emoto, a Japanese researcher and author, conducted studies that demonstrated that human consciousness and emotions can influence the molecular structure of water, which in turn affects how ice crystals form.[7]

In one study of psychokinesis (the ability to move objects through mental focus alone), researchers placed a metal needle in a controlled environment. The participant, located several hundred miles away, was asked to focus their intention on the needle. The results showed that the needle's movement was statistically significant when compared to its movement when no participant was focusing their intentions on it.[8]

MIND-MATTER INTERACTION 2.0

While it may be interesting to slightly influence dice and electronic equipment, or move a needle with the mind, humans have far greater capabilities for mind-matter interaction. Many of these capabilities were understood in the past but have been either forgotten or overlooked by modern society.

For example, in his book *Autobiography of a Yogi,* the prominent Indian teacher and leader Paramahansa Yogananda shared numerous accounts of spiritual leaders exhibiting supernatural abilities (referred to as Siddhis), such as saints who could instantly travel from one location to another or appear in two places simultaneously, and yogis who could become invisible at will.[9] The Bhagavad Gita, often considered one of the most important

Dolores Cannon
reported that some
of her hypnosis
clients shared
experiences of
being on ET ships
and provided
detailed information
about how the
ships operate and
navigate.

scriptures in Hinduism, also discusses yogis with similar supernatural abilities.[10]

As we will discuss further in Chapter 13, the "high technology" of the sites and hieroglyphics in ancient Egypt and similar sacred sites around the world also suggests the use of mental or conscious manipulation of physical objects and matter. This is one way that ancient peoples might have been able to carve extremely large granite blocks to precision and move them hundreds of miles.

One final example of the possibilities of mind-matter interaction is the phenomenon known as remote viewing. This occurs when a person obtains information about a distant or unseen location using intuitive insight, or extrasensory perception, without relying on physical senses or equipment. Accounts from many people claiming to have used remote viewing to gather information about distant or unseen targets reveal astonishing details.

The United States Army initiated remote viewing efforts in the early 1970s, as part of the Stargate Project. The targets were military installations and foreign bases, where objects were often hidden from sight, and the goal was to identify and determine if the objects had any potential military uses. After the Stargate Project was terminated in 1995, a final report indicated that, while there were some successes, the overall results were mixed.[11] However, other controlled studies of remote viewing have shown more consistent and positive results.[12,13]

The Future of Human Mind-Matter Interaction

To understand what we are capable of regarding mind-related technological advancements, we will need help from our galactic neighbors. In her book *The Custodians*, Dolores Cannon reported that some of her hypnosis clients shared experiences of being on ET ships and provided detailed information about how the ships operate and navigate. Central to the ships' operation is the integrated use of mental and mechanical systems with a form of thought projection that enables ETs to control their ships.

In addition, the ETs' advanced telepathy allows them to "sense" their surroundings and navigate through space using their conscious direction. As a result, their ships travel faster than the speed of light—at the speed of thought.

A common theme among ET and Star Nations when describing space travel is their knowledge and ability to transcend the conventional limitations of space and time. One way they do this is by utilizing energy manipulation techniques, such as altering their ships' energy fields, to create a form of propulsion that fundamentally differs from our understanding of physics and enables travel beyond the speed of light.

Another method ETs use to transcend the limits of space and time is to navigate through alternate dimensions or parallel realities to access distant locations almost instantaneously. For example, the ET Bashar, communicating through Darryl Anka, explained a method called "interdimensional travel" or "instantaneous travel":

> While you think of an object existing in a location, to us, location is one of the properties of the object. If you thus then have an object at point A and you isolate it with an energy bubble. In a sense unlock it from any particular reality, and thus then impose upon it the vibrational signature frequency of location B. It must stop existing in location A and instantaneously start taking up residence at

location B without actually having traveled the intervening distance. You have actually changed the locational variable in its energy signature.[14]

To a large extent, consciousness creates our reality. As the previous chapters have shown, we can become aware of different dimensions and realities and, with practice, move in and out of them, experience their nuances, and explore life beyond the veil. Someday we might even learn to alter our physical reality to routinely accomplish things that are currently beyond our wildest imagination, as in ancient Egypt or in space travel. However, there are a few more things we must learn in order to move forward.

CHAPTER NINE

UNITY CONSCIOUSNESS: THE NEXT STAGE IN HUMAN DEVELOPMENT

"Imagine all the people living life in peace."
—John Lennon

The term "unity consciousness" is relatively new and gaining popularity—most likely because humanity is moving in the direction of unity and love, as mentioned in Chapter 7. Unity consciousness can be a cringeworthy term for some because it challenges our ideas of individuality, making our ego defenses go up. It represents a dramatic shift from the current paradigm of power, money, fear, and greed. Looking at the news today, it is almost impossible to imagine how we could achieve unity consciousness, but according to many sources, the process has already begun.

What Is Unity Consciousness?

There are many descriptions of unity consciousness—authors have been writing about it for millennia—and it is hard to find a short and precise definition. The following is my definition of unity consciousness; other authors offer further nuances:

> Unity consciousness is the awareness of the interconnectedness among all living things and, through that, promotes love, empathy, and compassion. In addition, by transcending the false sense of separation among them, individuals can see themselves as part of a greater whole, which leads to a more profound sense of purpose and meaning in life.

Deepak Chopra writes about unity consciousness and draws parallels between it and quantum physics, suggesting that our understanding of reality can expand when we recognize we are all interconnected. Mindfulness teacher and Zen master Thich Nhat Hanh's work teaches that awareness can lead to compassionate action. Author and spiritual teacher Don Miguel Ruiz emphasizes personal freedom through awareness of our interconnectedness.

How Do We Experience Unity?

The first step in experiencing unity consciousness is to explore any resistance we may have to the idea. Possibly the most misunderstood component of unity is the loss of our identity and individuality. Our shields go up to protect our ego when we perceive a threat. We all want to feel special and unique, and the fear of losing that can evoke strong emotions.

However, unity does not mean the dissolution of individuality. Think about your hand. You have five distinct fingers, but they all join to form your hand. If one of the fingers goes missing, your hand is less effective, but it is still a hand. Similarly, when you are working on a puzzle, if a piece is missing, no other piece can take the place of the missing one, and your eye goes right to the gap in the puzzle until you find the piece and put it in place to complete the image.

A real-life example of unity comes from a friend of mine who lives in Asheville, North Carolina. In September 2024, a rare and powerful hurricane hit the area, causing massive devastation. For months after, my friend and I talked about how the cleanup was going. He consistently told me stories of how people within the community and nationwide banded together to provide money, resources, and time to help rebuild. While the resources were greatly appreciated, he said the feeling of togetherness and support from people giving of their time, sharing their homes, and spending time with traumatized people brought people to tears of joy and love.

Another example of oneness is an athletic team. Consider a football team that wants to win a championship. To do so, each player must flawlessly play their respective offensive or defensive position; the unified team is not made up of only quarterbacks or receivers. This misunderstanding is the basis of some people's resistance to unity; it is, of course, nonsense.

The magnificence of our hands, the beauty of a puzzle, and the magic of a team or community working together are unity consciousness. We can experience unity with God/Source in the same way we pierce the veil—through natural sensitivities, trauma, study, meditative states, near-death experiences, and the use of psychedelics (see Chapter 6). With all these methods, we are able to get a glimpse of reality outside of our three-dimensional box and experience divine connection.

"Oneness within
ourselves can only
be understood when
we go down into
the dungeons of
our shadow selves;
observe, acknowledge,
and eventually
integrate those parts of
ourselves back
into the bigger parts
of our Self."

—*Mary Schnorrenberg*

Unity consciousness does not mean that we have to be best friends with everyone we meet, agree with them on all subjects, or take no action if someone is involved in hurtful behavior. What it does mean is that we treat others as we would like to be treated and respect others as we want to be respected.

> "The problem with the world is that
> we draw the circle of our family too small."
> —*Mother Teresa*

The bottom line is that if we want to experience more unity in our life, we must focus on seeing more unity and, as Mother Teresa encouraged, "Be the change you wish to see in the world."

Unity and Our Shadow Selves

There are positive and negative sides to pursuing unity consciousness. It engenders feelings of acceptance, unconditional love, togetherness, and peace. However, to fully embrace feelings of unity with others, we must first be united within ourselves. This includes embracing parts of us that we hide from the outside world, and even from ourselves. They are the things we do and the desires or emotions we feel that we believe are socially unacceptable, are uncomfortable, or conflict with how we would like to see ourselves and how we want others to see us. The Swiss psychologist Carl Jung identified this as the "shadow self" and taught that personal growth is dependent on seeing and reconciling with this side of ourselves. Author Mary Schnorrenberg explained, "Oneness within ourselves can only be understood when we go down into the dungeons of our shadow selves; observe, acknowledge, and eventually integrate those parts of ourselves back into the bigger parts of our Self."[1]

The shadow self is a critical step in another aspect of awakening. This will be discussed along with ways to address your shadow in Chapter 15.

Separation

We live in a world that is steeped in separation, the opposite of unity. Just as a fish may not be aware that it lives in a pond, we are not naturally aware that we live in a three-dimensional physical environment of separation. In our defense, we live in physical bodies that are separate from others' bodies. There is a "me" and "you," and an "us" and "them." We are told that we are special, and not only are others not like us, they also may not like us because we are not like them. Most organized religion teaches that we are separate from God/Source. We have a tendency to feel separated from others—as a result of binary opposition, our dimensions, our evolutionary past, solar and astrological cycles, and our biological development—but this perspective may be changing.

Binary opposition or dualism is the idea that the opposite of something must exist in order for us to understand what it is (e.g., light/dark, black/white, good/evil). In this perspective, we are experiencing separation so that we can better understand oneness. One path to growth is understanding that we are more connected to God/Source than we have ever dreamed.

The dimension we live in provides a natural experience of separation. The third dimension is inherently physical, so humans and other life forms are contained in separate bodies. In addition, according to Barbara Hand Clow's dimensional model, we are consciously in the fourth dimension, which is like a canopy surrounding us, acting like a lens that creates separation and duality (see Chapter 5). When we pierce the veil, especially through meditation, near-death experiences, and psychedelic drugs, we can escape our world of separation and experience glimpses of oneness. As we evolve to higher dimensions, our resident state will be oneness, and we will have to work at slowing down our vibrations, in a sense, to pierce the veil from the other side, to interact with those still in the third dimension.

Our evolutionary past suggests that we evolved from simpler creatures. Early humans operated with a fight-or-flight and fear mentality. In a primitive and dangerous environment, early humans had to fight off competitors. Food was scarce, predatory animals were always lurking in the bushes, and other humans living nearby were competing for the same resources. This perspective is still very much in play today; whether it is true or not, we are told that other countries or groups are out to get us and take away our wealth, food, or safety. Thus, we fall back on our evolutionary history and separate ourselves from one another.

However, humanistic psychologists like Abraham Maslow and Carl Rogers believed that humans have an innate drive to achieve social, cognitive, and emotional growth and self-actualization. This means that humanity may naturally adopt unity as the next step in our evolution as a species and move away from fear, division, and self-preservation.

Solar and astrological cycles could be another reason we experience separation. While they don't explain humanity's history of separation, the Earth's precessional cycle and astrological transits offer possible explanations for how external forces may be currently influencing us to move from separation to oneness.

"Humanity wants to
reach for the stars
but very often
cannot even reach
for the hand
of its neighbor."

—*Germane, channeled
through Lyssa Royal Holt*

"Humanity wants to reach for the stars but very often cannot even reach for the hand of its neighbor."
—*Germane, channeled through Lyssa Royal Holt*

Our biological development may also be a factor in our separation. I have always been fascinated by the concept of perspective taking in human development. Perspective taking is the ability to understand that another person may not have the same perspective or understanding as we do. Swiss psychologist Jean Piaget developed a theory of cognitive development that suggests that perspective taking begins in the concrete operational stage of childhood, which typically ranges from ages seven to twelve.

He tested his theory with children in the well-known Three Mountain Task. In this test, he created a three-dimensional model that contained mountains of various sizes; one mountain was smaller than the other two. He then positioned three children around the sides of the table on which the model was built, placed a doll or a building in various places on the model, and asked the children to predict what the other children would see. Many participants under the age of around seven years said that the other children would be able to see what they could see, even though one of the taller mountains was blocking their view.

This means that until around the age of seven, the human brain struggles to understand that other people may not perceive the world in the same way that we do. My point is that our strong inclination to see ourselves as separate from others and God/Source may be a cognitive development factor, similar to perspective taking. Perhaps part of our maturity and advancement into higher consciousness in a New Earth reality will be to develop the ability to understand that we are not separate individuals but are, in reality, all one.

Experiential Exercises to Experience Unity and Oneness

SET POSITIVE ATTITUDES

Practicing an attitude of gratitude, thankfulness, and peace helps raise our vibration so we can experience and be a light to others. As Hand Clow suggested, one way to maintain a level of love and unity in everyday situations is to consider both perspectives.

INCREASE YOUR VIBRATIONAL LEVELS

As we increase our vibrational levels, we move from experiencing separation to unity, love, and connectedness. We can do this through meditation or the use of psychedelic drugs. Many guided meditations focus on oneness. Hand Clow's nine-dimension meditation series in Chapter 5 and Scott Taylor's near-death experience meditations in Chapter 6 are excellent ways to experience the higher dimensions of oneness. Several psychedelic drugs can also help us achieve altered states of consciousness that include powerful experiences of oneness.

NOTE: Please consult a physician or therapist before using these techniques. Always make sure to practice meditations, intentions, and exercises in an environment where it is safe to do so. Do not engage in these activities while driving a car or operating any kind of machinery.

CHAPTER TEN

OUR DIVINE NATURE

"In the vastness of the universe, we are not separate;
we are expressions of a single consciousness."
—*Alan Watts*

In the previous two chapters, I discussed consciousness as it relates to other people and our physical world. Now we will delve deeper into the nature of our consciousness—here referred to as "the soul"—in relation to God/Source. For the purposes of this book, the working definition of a soul is the essence of a living being, the seat of consciousness, emotions, character, and identity. It transcends the physical body and continues to exist beyond physical death.

The core debate surrounding our divine nature is whether we, as souls, are separate from God/Source (dualism) or connected to and a part of God/Source (nonduality). Most organized religions' core doctrines teach that we are one with the Divine; however, either intentionally or not, they teach that we are separate from the Divine, in many cases needing to appease a vengeful Almighty or seek salvation from punishment. With the current awakening, we are moving beyond the fear-based components of religions toward oneness and unity.

"The total
number of
minds in the
Universe is one."

—*Erwin Schrödinger*

"Enlightenment is when a wave realizes it is the ocean."
—*Thich Nhat Hanh*

Psychology generally focuses on observable behavior and mental processes and does not provide much information about the soul. However, the founders of psychology knew there was something beyond our physical senses and described it in different ways. For example, Sigmund Freud proposed the concept of the id; Carl Jung introduced the concept of the psyche, the possibility of angels, and the idea that the mind exists outside of the body; and William James explored consciousness and experience. Philosophers have been divided for centuries on the subject of souls. Plato, Aristotle, and René Descartes believed in an eternal soul, while others like David Hume and Immanuel Kant did not believe in eternal existence.

Determining whether a soul exists is obviously outside of the capabilities of present-day science because a soul cannot be observed or measured in a laboratory. One attempt was made in 1907 to measure the weight of a soul. Dr. Duncan MacDougall experimented with six dying patients, weighing them at the precise time of their death. According to MacDougall, one patient lost twenty-one grams of weight the moment they died. Many scientists dismissed this study as methodologically flawed because it only involved a small test sample of six patients. The study inspired the critically acclaimed movie *21 Grams* (2003), starring Sean Penn and Naomi Watts.

The nondualism of the soul is not a revolutionary idea in religion; it has been taught in Hinduism, Buddhism, Taoism, Christianity, and Indigenous spiritual traditions for centuries. The prolific Buddhist monk Thich Nhat Hanh said, "We are here to awaken from the illusion of our separateness."[1]

Christian mystic Richard Rohr echoed this: "Nonduality is the highest level of consciousness. It is the mind that can accept paradox and mystery, and it is the mind that can live with ambiguity."[2]

Where Does the Soul Come From?

While psychologists, philosophers, and scientists debate the existence of the soul, religious followers attribute the creation of the soul to the higher power of their faith. Most of the world's approximately 4,200 organized religions believe in a soul that lives forever and was created by a divine source such as God, Yahweh, or Allah. The unity of God and humans is discussed in the religious texts of many faith traditions:

- Christianity teaches that the Kingdom of God is within us. Mystics like Meister Eckhart and St. John of the Cross spoke of union with God.

- Buddhism teaches that we are all part of an intricate and interconnected universe.

- Hinduism teaches that individual souls (Atman) are a part of Brahma, the foundation of all things, unchanging and eternal.

- Islam teaches that the soul comes directly from Allah.

- Mystical Judaism (Kabbalah) describes divine energy flowing into the physical world to create the physical world and human souls.

"The total number of minds in the Universe is one."
—*Erwin Schrödinger*

However, not all religions teach that we are a part of the Divine, and even among those that do, beliefs about the soul and many other religious and theological topics vary considerably within them. For example, as of 2024, there are approximately forty-five thousand distinct Christian denominations worldwide.[3]

Separation from God/Source

Separation from God/Source significantly affects our spiritual awakening. The illusion of separation is a strong and consistent theme throughout *A Course in Miracles*, written by Helen Schucman channeling Jesus. The core teaching is that separation from God/Source, other people, and our true selves is a fundamental illusion of humanity and the cause of all suffering. We are bombarded with messages and teachings that promote feelings of fear, guilt, and isolation, which reinforce the illusion. To combat the illusion, we must practice remembering the reality of our oneness with God/Source, others, and our true selves.

We feel separate from God/Source for some of the same reasons we feel separate from one another. We may have been taught this separation growing up in our religious traditions. In many religions, we are told that God is up in heaven, and we are down here on Earth. Only spiritual leaders can intervene and bestow sacred teachings on us. Additionally, many Protestant denominations teach "worm theology," the idea that we are born as worthless sinners, separated from God, and in need of salvation.

"This identity as a separate self seemed so real that it seemed very difficult to find God. ... One very effective way in my return is to remember to see the Christ in all my brothers, to see the Light of God in them, to see the truth about them."

—Rev. Mary M. Mohan

Religions may teach separation from the Divine because the organization seeks power and control over its followers. These groups disparage ideas or practices that promote direct contact with God, including prayer, which they say should be left to religious leaders. One way to promote separation is to instill fear and portray God as judgmental, thereby encouraging followers to rely on religious leaders for guidance and redemption.

We also feel separate from God/Source because we live in the third and fourth dimensions, immersed in separation. It is all around us; we are time-bound, have limited perceptions of our world, and feel a strong sense of separation from many things, including ourselves and God/Source. We can move beyond this shroud of separation, but it takes practice.

From a dimensional perspective, the fourth dimension is like a canopy surrounding us. As higher energies slow down to enter the fourth dimension, it acts like a lens that creates separation and duality: light/dark, good/bad, self/other. According to Barbara Hand Clow, humanity has not been a good caretaker of our earthly dimensions, and—possibly as a result of this or because we are ready to evolve—we are collectively moving into the fifth and higher dimensions and adopting a unity consciousness.

"This identity as a separate self seemed so real that it seemed very difficult to find God. But the good news is I am learning to let go of this false identity. I am willing to open to my one Self and let my mind be healed of all its false ideas. One very effective way in my return is to remember to see the Christ in all my brothers, to see the Light of God in them, to see the truth about them."
—Rev. Mary M. Mohan, from A Course in Miracles *Workbook Insights*, Lesson 160 [4]

Reconnecting with Our Divine Nature

While the idea of being unified with God/Source is not uni-laterally accepted within religious circles, it is common among people in the metaphysical and modern-day spir-itual communities. In the first book in Neale Donald Walsch's *Conversations with God* series, he presented a met-aphor: God shattered himself like a mirror into trillions of pieces to create all the living things of the universe. Each piece is an individual soul reflecting the Divine and thus carries a part of the whole within it. Similarly, the Kabbalah explains that God created the universe by con-tracting his infinite light to an infinite density and energy and then exploded himself out into all directions so that every part of the universe contains the essence of God.

A third metaphor for our divine connection is a holo-gram. A hologram is a two-dimensional picture that uses special light techniques to create an image that looks three-dimensional. The light passing through or reflecting off each tiny portion of the holographic plate reconstructs the whole image. So, even if you cut a small piece from the hologram, that piece still has the light wave information to re-create the entire image. It's like ripping up a picture of a flower, with all the fragments containing the image of the complete flower. In this way, every part of the uni-verse, including us, contains the totality of God/Source.

A fourth metaphor for our intimate relationship with God/Source is a fractal, a never-ending pattern that repeats itself. Every part of a fractal looks very similar to the whole image, regardless of how large or small it is. For example, the complex pattern of a snowflake is a fractal; a close-up view of its arms and branches mirrors its overall shape. God/Source consciousness is the primary force or source of all existence. This consciousness manifests in the physical world by fractalizing its energy. As the energy is fractalized, it creates the diverse and complex structures we observe in the physical world. This implies that everything in the universe is interconnected and a part of one Source, one Spirit, one God.

Matías De Stefano describes returning to unity with God/Source as the only goal for every living being. In his dimensional model, the first dimension is the first thought before anything was created. It is the "I Am" consciousness. It contains no forms, no light, nothing. It is a void whose only characteristic is feeling. Lyssa Royal Holt calls it "The Golden Lake." It is when I Am thought, "What else can I become?" that the universe was created. De Stefano explains that in order for us to return to I Am we have to forget everything we have learned about reality. It is only then that we can experience the unity of oneness with God/Source.[5]

When we experience a deep divine connection, it is the final step in awareness of reality, our existence, and enlightenment. To experience it, we can ask God/Source to help us adjust our perspective to see our divine connection. You can also try the following meditation.

Experiential Exercise: Who Are You Meditation

You have a name, an address, and a family. Maybe you are tall or short, have brown hair or blonde hair. There are many things that make you unique, but you are much more than that—something that many of us miss. To see what I mean by this, I invite you to read through the following visualization and then close your eyes and experience it for yourself.

Imagine you are in a large, darkened room. In front of you is a long, narrow table with a black tablecloth extending to your right and left. Now, one by one, in your mind's eye, place everything on the table that makes you who you are in this life. You may want to start with your name, age, gender, address, and date of birth. You can also add the schools you went to; your driver's license, profession, and educational degrees; or that you are a father, mother, son, daughter, husband, or wife. Take some time with this so you don't miss anything that makes you who you are or distinguishes you from all others.

Now, after you have placed everything that defines you on the table, what is left? Who is standing there looking at all of these items? Some might say that there is nothing standing there because a person is the sum total of all the things that define them; others might say the timeless essence of a person remains, their consciousness or infinite soul.

Spend some time in this space, remembering that you are not the items and attributes on the table. Now, turn around so your back is to the table. You are now looking into nothingness. There is no form, no images, no thought, no sound. Be present in this moment.

This is the All That Is, Source, the Eternal Consciousness of the Universe. It is God without all the religious trappings.

Picture yourself being enveloped in this nothingness—like a drop of water falling back into the ocean. Stay in this state for several moments; feel the warm love, the feel of home, and the expansiveness of being a part of everything. Feel the intense and profound peace. This is what eternal reality feels like.

When you are ready, turn back toward the table with all the items you placed on it. The moment you do this, you are projecting your consciousness into the physical world. You are fractalizing your divine energy and re-creating the hologram of this life and this time.

You can now see how "unreal" these things that you think make you Who you are really are. They are a projection—very real to you in this time, but still just a projection. It is just like waking up from a vivid dream that moments before was very real to you.

After sitting with these thoughts and emotions for some time, slowly and gently come back to your awakened state, knowing that anytime you wish you can return.

This is how we can see beyond the chaos, unrest, and hatred, and return to peace and love—the only truly real things in the universe.

"Nothing real can be threatened. Nothing unreal exists. Herein lies the peace of God."
—A Course in Miracles

A Healing Process

Once you experience your divine nature and can look back at your life and see it as a projection and illusion, you're done. That's it. You can learn things from teachers, astrologers, oracles, or religious leaders, but you do not need them. You humbly know where you came from; you know Who you are.

This is also one part of the healing process. As you disconnect from the parts of you that are not real and embrace your true divinity, you are complete. You can go in peace to fulfill whatever tasks you feel called to do, without fear and full of love and compassion for anyone who comes into your life.

CHAPTER ELEVEN

COMING HOME

"There's no place like home."
—The Wizard of Oz *(1939)*

I once read that *home* is the most emotionally charged word in every language. The idea of home carries enormous emotional weight because it conveys much more than just a physical place; it conveys safety, security, memories, love, relationships, and emotional well-being, with parallels to a womb experience. It's the closest experience we can have to unconditional love. We will always yearn for home, even if we have not had a positive home life in this lifetime.

God/Source is our eternal Home. Many of us have been longing for this Home for as long as we can remember. This longing may have shown up as a passion for religion and spirituality, and then further developed into an interest in spiritual practices and working with psychics, mediums, angels, and ETs. Or perhaps you looked into a starry night sky and felt a distant beckoning. You wanted to draw closer but were unsure and a little afraid.

Each chapter of this book has been a breadcrumb leading you Home, to your divine nature—from experiencing different dimensions, to identifying ways to pierce the veil and learning how unity consciousness is a precursor to contact with our galactic family.

"I am in Heaven now. I am still as God created me. But I am still not aware of my Home as long as I choose to believe in separation. With the power of my mind, I experience a world of bodies and have forgotten my true Identity as an extension of God. Now I would reverse that. I would practice reinforcing the truth instead of the ego's lies."

—Rev. Mary M. Mohan

"You've all gone to sleep in heaven and are dreaming."
—*Bashar, channeled through Darryl Anka*

There is one very important difference between being separated from our physical home and feeling separated from our spiritual Home. When we leave our physical home, we are physically not there. Conversely, while we may not always feel our spiritual Home, we have never left it.

We Never Left

Once we understand Who we really are and accept and experience our divine connection, we are Home. As the guided meditation in Chapter 10 reminded us, when we experience our divine origin, apart from everything we associate with "us" in this life, we are Home.

Once we remember we are already Home, the higher dimensions of unconditional love, unity, and togetherness can be a normal experience for us. This is not easy at first; it does not come naturally, but by consistently reinforcing our thoughts and asking for help from God/Source, we will see and feel our mind changing.

> "I am in Heaven now. I am still as God created me. But I am still not aware of my Home as long as I choose to believe in separation. With the power of my mind, I experience a world of bodies and have forgotten my true Identity as an extension of God. Now I would reverse that. I would practice reinforcing the truth instead of the ego's lies."
> —*Rev. Mary M. Mohan, from* A Course in Miracles Workbook Insights, *Lesson 202*[1]

We never left our divine Home; we are in heaven with God right now, even as we experience this temporary physical life. And while we experience our oneness at times, we are here to learn and appreciate all the wonder and beauty of this world, knowing that we can always return Home at any time.

The Next Step—Getting to Know Our Galactic Neighborhood

In light of the shift and awakening to a new world and returning Home, several sources state that when humanity shifts to higher consciousness and manifests widespread cooperation, kindness, unity, and support, it will initiate the First Contact. This means that as our overall frequency increases, we will become compatible and able to interact openly with beings from other planets. Earth will officially and practically become a member of the neighborhood of planets, with open and active interaction with the other planets and their inhabitants. Section 3 will introduce you to our galactic neighborhood and provide ways to begin your connection with them.

AWAKENING TO OUR PLACE IN THE UNIVERSE

CHAPTER TWELVE

DO THEY OR DON'T THEY EXIST?

"To believe without questioning or to dismiss without
investigation is to behave unscientifically."
—*Margaret Mead, former president of the Association
of the Advancement of Science*

You don't have to believe in life on other planets, unidentified flying objects (UFOs), unidentified anomalous phenomena (UAPs), or ETs. Nothing bad will happen if you think the stories, reports, and video clips are fake or the reports are suspect. It is certainly justifiable not to believe, since we don't have active communications or interactions with civilizations from other planets—at least not on a large scale.

But suppose ETs do exist and are capable of space travel; they are likely much older and more technologically advanced than we are. They may have been involved with our planet, undetected by design, helping us behind the scenes for thousands of years. According to a 2021 Pew Research Center study of 10,417 adults in the United States, most respondents believed that intelligent life exists on other planets but were almost evenly split on whether UFOs are a threat (Figure 6). Most of those surveyed also believed that the reports of UFO sightings by military personnel are evidence of ET life.[1]

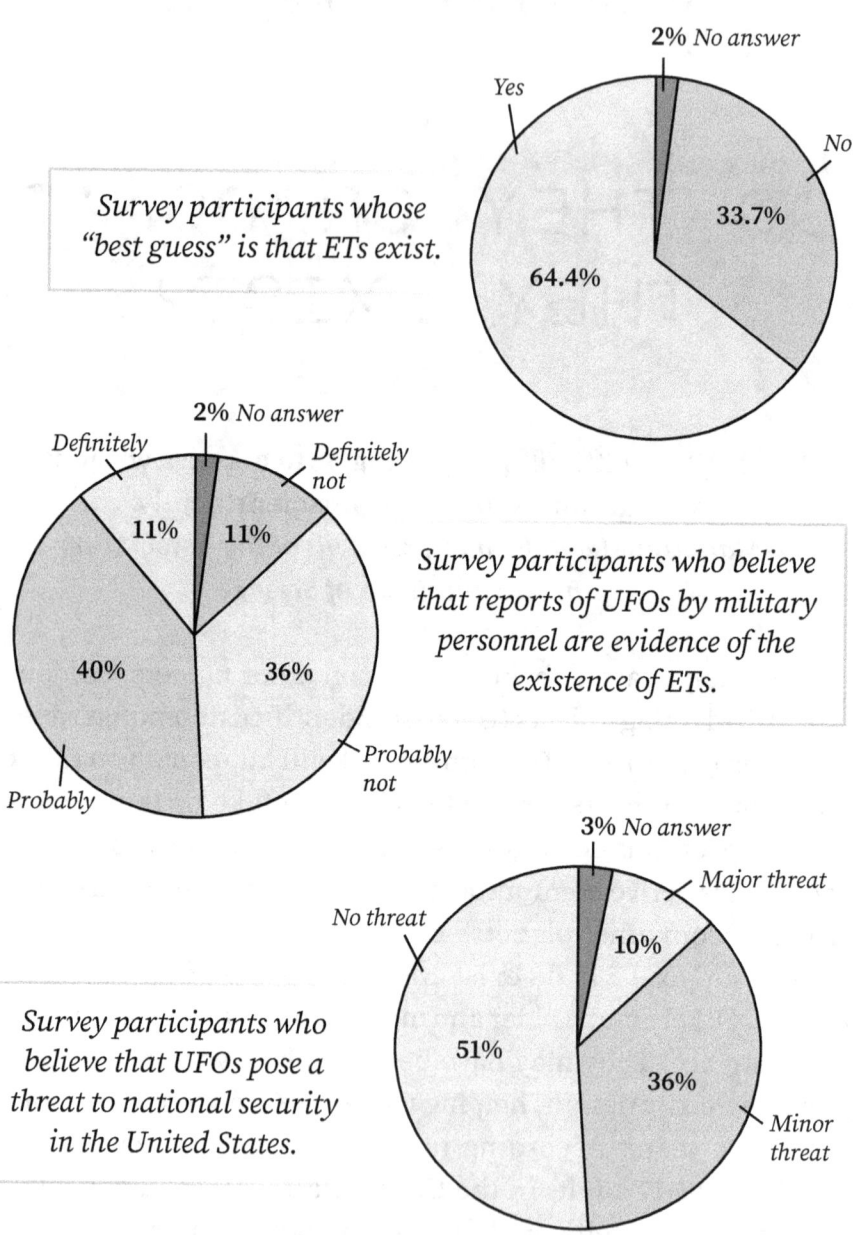

Survey participants whose "best guess" is that ETs exist.

Survey participants who believe that reports of UFOs by military personnel are evidence of the existence of ETs.

Survey participants who believe that UFOs pose a threat to national security in the United States.

Figure 6. A summary of the results of a 2021 Pew Research Center study on Americans' opinions about ETs and UFOs.

In this chapter and the next, we will explore two questions: Is there intelligent life on other planets? And, if ETs do exist, why are they not openly interacting with us? The starting point in this discussion relates to your strategy for determining what you believe to be true. Are you tied to scientific materialism or open to information received through other sources? While there are thousands of reports of UAPs—government reports, so-called abduction stories, Area 51 speculations, unexplained crop circles, and mysterious ancient archaeological sites—as you will see, most information about our galactic neighborhood comes from channeled sources.

Official Reports

In August 1977, a radio telescope at Ohio State University detected a thirty-seven-second pulse of radiation near the constellation Sagittarius, known as the "Wow!" signal.[2] The origin of this pulse remains a mystery, with potential explanations ranging from a large astronomical event to transmissions from intelligent life.

In February 2003, Search for Extraterrestrial Intelligence (SETI) astronomers reexamined two hundred areas of the sky for unexplained radio signals. They discovered that all had vanished except one, which had grown stronger. The signal originates from a location between Pisces and Aries, where no known stars or planets exist, and it resonates at a frequency associated with hydrogen, the universe's most abundant element. Some researchers believe this frequency could be a deliberate choice by intelligent ETs attempting to communicate and offers strong support of ET contact.[3]

In 2022 NASA established a panel to explain its work on UAPs. The following May, during a public meeting, the panel reported that after reviewing eight hundred mysterious sightings that had occurred over decades, sixteen to forty of the sightings had been deemed "possibly really anomalous." The panel also mentioned that in its investigation, it found that "commercial pilots are very reluctant to report sightings because of the stigma surrounding flying saucers."[4]

In November 2024, the Pentagon and the Director of National Intelligence released an annual report on UAP sightings that included seven hundred new cases that occurred from May 2023 to June 2024. The report stated that the new information did not confirm ET life. However, twenty-one cases could not be explained. Interestingly, those twenty-one sightings occurred near national security sites and were recorded on video, had multiple eyewitnesses, or were captured by other sensors.[5]

Also in November 2024, members of the US Congress held a joint hearing by subcommittees of the House Oversight Committee titled "Unidentified Anomalous Phenomena: Exposing the Truth." Tim Gallaudet, retired rear admiral, US Navy, and CEO of Ocean STL Consulting, LLC, testified that during a pre-deployment exercise off the East Coast, he received an email from one of the participating Navy F/A-18 jet pilots containing what is referred to as the "Go Fast" video. It had recorded an unidentified object exhibiting flight and structural characteristics unlike anything in the US arsenal. Gallaudet said, "The very next day, the email disappeared from my account and those of the other recipients without explanation."[6]

During his testimony, Luis Elizondo, author and former Department of Defense official, wrote, "Let me be clear. UAP are real. Advanced technologies not made by our government—or any other government—are monitoring sensitive military installations around the globe."[7] He said that the

United States has obtained UAP technologies, as have some of our adversaries.

Elizondo also testified that the United States had established secret UAP crash retrieval programs to identify and reverse engineer alien craft. When asked who was developing these advanced technologies, Elizondo replied that neither the United States nor any other government was responsible, but rather that private companies, including those with nonhuman intelligence, might be involved.

Michael Gold, a former NASA associate administrator of space policy and partnerships and a member of the NASA UAP Independent Study Team, stated that the damaging stigma surrounding UAPs continues to block scientific dialogue and hinder open discussions. "As the saying goes, the truth is out there," Gold said. "We just need to be bold enough and brave enough to face it."[8]

Government Cover-Ups

Many people suspect that the US government has not released all the information it has regarding UAPs and ETs to the public. Of the many reports of government cover-ups, the case of David Grusch stands out as a credible example.

Grusch served as an intelligence officer in the Air Force for more than fourteen years and earned numerous awards for his participation in covert American security operations. In 2023 Grusch and his attorney, who served as the original Intelligence Community Inspector General, filed a complaint through the whistleblowers' protocol within the Department of Defense (DoD). In the complaint, Grusch stated that he was subject to illegal retaliation for reporting on a covert materials recovery program that had obtained intact and partially intact craft of nonhuman origin. He and others noted that these vehicles had unusual shapes and were made of materials with uncommon atomic structures that emitted distinctive radiation patterns. In addition, he claimed that government teams were seeking to reverse engineer these crafts' components. His complaint stated that the information he provided on these subjects was illegally withheld from Congress.

Grusch also reported that for decades the Air Force has operated disinformation campaigns to discredit reported sightings of unexplained objects in order to avoid congressional oversight of UAP programs. He stated that the United States has possibly been aware of nonhuman activity since the 1930s.[9] As a result of Grusch's complaint, government-run investigations were initiated and a few UAP working groups were formed. The Pentagon and DoD have consistently denied Grusch's allegations and any verifiable information about nonhuman vehicles or reverse engineering programs.[10]

Another creditable statement related to government cover-ups of ET contact was made by retired Air Force Intelligence Officer Richard Doty in 2017. He admitted, on camera, that military personnel conducting unacknowledged special access projects stage alien abductions to lay the psychological foundation for an interplanetary conflict in the near future.

> We did do that, yes. The Office of Special Investigations did that. There was a special group out of the 76th 2nd intel wing at Fort Belvoir that came out and did that. They had these people that had maybe some sort of defects, anatomical defects that were brought in to fool people into thinking they were aliens. I can't give you any specifics because the program is still classified.

They're probably still doing it. I wouldn't doubt they're still doing it.[11]

Finally, on September 9, 2025, the US House Committee convened a hearing titled "Restoring Public Trust through UAP Transparency and Whistleblower Protection."[12] During the proceedings, four individuals—representing both the private sector and the military—testified under oath regarding multiple encounters with UAPs. Several of these incidents were corroborated by multiple witnesses and verified through electronic surveillance systems. Reported sightings included Tic Tac–shaped objects, a glowing red square, massive rectangular crafts, and a large orb of blue and white light that pulsed rhythmically and maneuvered with the erratic grace of a butterfly.

While the testimonies themselves were striking, they were eclipsed by the accounts of severe retaliation against those who reported these encounters. Witnesses described intimidation by superiors and unidentified individuals, who allegedly warned them not to speak publicly or report their experiences. Consequences ranged from job termination to blacklisting across government agencies. One witness, after agreeing to an interview with George Knapp, chief investigative reporter for KLAS-TV in Las Vegas, was visited by two men in suits. They cautioned her against sharing her story, stating, "It's a big desert out there. It would be a shame if anything happened to either of you." She feared not only for her own safety but also for the safety of her daughter.

"As I sit before you today, I and many other whistleblowers have no job prospects and no foreseeable professional future in a nation all of us came forward to defend."
—*Dylan Borland, former 1N1 geospatial intelligence specialist for the US Air Force*[13]

Unofficial Reports

For those of you who would like to read more about crash retrieval programs and other unofficial covert military programs and findings, Ryan S. Wood offers two excellent books to consider. Wood is a prolific researcher and second-generation ufologist, and he is considered a leading authority on the top secret, classified Majestic-12 intelligence documents and the 1941 Cape Girardeau, Missouri, UFO crash, among others. These extensive reports support claims of early government involvement in ET encounters, including covert investigations, recovered alien craft, and suppressed evidence—long before Roswell became well known.

Wood's first book, *Majic Eyes Only: Earth's Encounters with Extraterrestrial Technology,* reviews over one hundred UFO crash retrievals, along with authenticity discussions of many of the Majestic documents. His second book, *The AI Ufologist: Answering the Big Questions of Ufology,* addresses thirty sophisticated and complex questions, including the rationale behind governmental secrecy on UFO matters and the intricate balance between national security and the pursuit of knowledge. It also explores humanity's potential response to ET threats and the involvement of private companies in ufology and space exploration.

Sacred Sites

Ancient sacred sites around the world offer windows into what civilizations were like thousands of years ago. These include Machu Picchu in Peru, known as the lost city of the Incas; the mysterious Stonehenge in England; and the dozens of pyramids and temples in the Americas, Turkey, and Egypt. Many of these sites are architectural wonders that have baffled scientists and engineers for hundreds of years. Several contain references to specific constellations like Orion, the Pleiades, Ursa Major, and Draco.

For example, the temple of Hathor in Dendera, Egypt, is dedicated to a group of seven goddesses, or sisters; the lead sister, Hathor, is referred to as The Lady of Heaven. The seven Hathor sisters are associated with the seven suns of the Pleiades star cluster: Alcyone, Maia, Taygeta, Electra, Celaeno, Sterope, and Merope, also known as the Seven Sisters. In addition, the temple's design and hieroglyphic inscriptions point to a connection to the Pleiadian system. In the temple of Hathor, several of the walls and ceilings contain images depicting people reaching up to stars in front of a blue background. When the color blue appears in Egyptian temples, some archaeologists claim it refers to ETs. On the doorways going into the Holy of Holies, the site's most sacred room, the word *SABA* is embedded on the frame. Two symbols of the word *SABA*, which means "gateway to the stars," are used in the cover design of this book: the rectangle with an extra line on the top and sides refers to a gateway, and the star with the dot at its center signifies a civilization.

I had an extraordinary opportunity to tour Egypt in the fall of 2024. The extensive twelve-day tour spanned the Giza Plaza in Cairo and the many sacred sites in Luxor, Aswan, and Dashur. In addition to two archaeologist tour guides, the renowned Swiss author Erich von Däniken

"Can we still
afford to close our
eyes and stop up
our ears because new
ideas are supposed
to be heretical
and absurd?"

—*Erich von Däniken*

joined us for several days. An avid researcher of ET connections with ancient civilizations, he has authored more than thirty books on the subject. His most popular book, *Chariots of the Gods?*, was initially published in 1968, translated into twenty-eight languages, and sold over sixty million copies worldwide. The fiftieth anniversary edition was published in 2018 and includes updated information. Even at ninety years old, Däniken shares his extensive knowledge of countless archaeological sites around the world and his passion for researching connections to ET worlds through his compelling stories.

In *Chariots of the Gods?*, Däniken presented aerial photographs of images that look remarkably like airstrips seen from high above the ground; these designs could not have been created unless the image creators were several thousand feet off the ground. Additionally, Däniken included images from ancient sites of seemingly humanoid figures in versions of space suits, sitting in what looks remarkably like the cockpit of some craft with fire extending behind it.

Däniken also commented on what is extremely evident to anyone visiting the sites of ancient Egypt—what archaeologists call the "high technology" of these sites. They feature massive structures constructed from twenty-to-thirty-ton smooth blocks of solid granite made to exacting dimensions. Scientists have posited how Egyptians carved, moved, and assembled these buildings with primitive tools, but no one knows for certain how it was done. The ancient Egyptians might have used their conscious abilities to manipulate the stone with sound or vibration, or perhaps ETs were involved.

I was in awe when I stood next to Egypt's largest obelisk, which Queen Hatshepsut had constructed 3,500 years ago in the area of Karnak. This 100-foot monolith, carved out of a single slab of pink granite weighing approximately 350 tons, has polished, perfectly straight edges that vary only within fractions of an inch over the span of the column. Even more fascinating is that the obelisk was made in a quarry in Aswan and somehow moved 135 miles to the north to Karnak. No one knows how the ancient Egyptians made the obelisk or moved it—or how it could be done even now.

"If we want to set out on the arduous search for the truth, we must all summon up the courage to leave the lines along which we have thought until now and as the first step, begin to doubt everything that we previously accepted as correct and true. Can we still afford to close our eyes and stop up our ears because new ideas are supposed to be heretical and absurd?"
—*Erich von Däniken*[14]

Another notable author investigating sacred sites is Graham Hancock. Born in Scotland and a graduate of Durham University in England, Hancock has published several international bestsellers, including *The Sign and the Seal, Fingerprints of the Gods,* and *Heaven's Mirror.*[15] Hancock's work centers on ancient civilizations that appear to have had advanced knowledge of astronomy, engineering, mathematics, and consciousness, far beyond the capabilities of the native cultures. Graham suggests these civilizations were destroyed by a global cataclysmic event, possibly a comet impact, around twelve thousand years ago. The survivors of the event were able to pass on a portion of their knowledge to other civilizations. Hancock's work has been criticized by some traditional archaeologists and institutions, which is to be expected given that he challenges conventional thinking. As discussed in detail in Chapter 1, paradigm shifts are often initially rejected because, according to change theory, the first step in change is denial.

Hancock participated in a fascinating Netflix series, *Ancient Apocalypse,* produced by Bruce Kennedy and Clementine Mortelman.[16] In the series, he explored several archaeological sites around the world, including Malta's nineteen ancient temples. He showed that in addition to the extreme improbability of Stone Age hunter-gatherers fabricating and erecting several temples using twenty-to-thirty-ton megaliths, the builders would have had to possess an extraordinarily advanced understanding of the cosmos and engineering skills that surpass our current capabilities.

The most interesting feature of Malta's temples is their alignment to the sky. At first glance, none of the temples face the same direction, and only one (Mnajdra) is oriented to the solstices. This means that the rising sun's rays bisect Mnajdra's entrances during the spring and fall equinoxes (March 21 and September 21). At sunrise on the summer and winter solstices, the longest and shortest days of the year, a different light source illuminates the temple: the star Sirius. In ancient Egyptian culture, Sirius was associated with the goddess Isis, the daughter of the sky goddess Nut and the earth god Geb. She was married to her brother Osiris, the god of the afterlife.

None of the other eighteen Malta temples aligns with the solstices because they were all built at different times, centuries apart. Due to Earth's wobble in its axis, or precession, the view of the night sky changes over the years as constellations appear to shift position slowly, with a one-degree difference in the rising or setting position of any given star every seventy-two years. Software programs can rewind what the sky looked like thousands of years ago, and when

While there are
thousands of
reports of UAPs
and ETs, most of
the information
about our galactic
neighborhood
comes from
channeled sources.

these models of the ancient sky are overlaid on the temples of Malta, Sirius passes the entrances of all the temples at some point in time. So, Hancock hypothesized that each time Sirius shifted out of position, a new temple was built to align with the star. Hancock also showed that the temples are far older than the dates given by archaeologists of 5,600 and 4,500 years, possibly as old as 11,000 years.

Other authors and researchers are uncovering new information about possible ET influence on human history. A massive underground city was recently discovered through new technological imaging under the Giza Plaza in Egypt, where the pyramids of Khufu (The Great Pyramid), Khafre, and Menkaure stand. We await the additional information that will be revealed as a result of this discovery.

While ancient sacred sites do not prove that humans had assistance from ET teachers, architects, or builders, there is no scientific explanation of how primitive humans could have erected these extraordinary structures worldwide. What we have now are frequently updated hypotheses of these ongoing mysteries, with hints that point to the stars.

While there are thousands of reports of UAPs and ETs, most of the information about our galactic neighborhood comes from channeled sources.

Channeled Information

It is important to reiterate that humanity has been receiving and relying on channeled information for millennia. The sacred texts of all the world's religions were channeled through humans in some form, and we have been comfortable with this process. Likewise, the most detailed information about our galactic neighborhood comes from people who channel information from nonphysical sources. The main challenge in researching channeled information is that many people claim—both truthfully and fraudulently—to have connections with celestial sources, such as angels, spirits, nonphysical collectives, and ETs, making it difficult to discern whom to believe. I believe the most reasonable way to approach ET content is to focus on those who have been channeling specific sources for many years. This way, we have a better chance of weeding out charlatans, fraudsters, and scammers.

The following four channelers, all of whom we have already discussed in this book, are well respected: Dolores Cannon, Lyssa Royal Holt, and Barbara Hand Clow and Gerry Clow.

Cannon was an American author and hypnotherapist specializing in past-life regression. Her work centered on metaphysical topics, including reincarnation, ET life, and alternative realities. In her fascinating book *The Custodians* (1998), she reflected on more than twenty years of working with regressing clients with ET and UAP experiences. The book provides amazing details about ETs, where they come from, what they eat, how they communicate, whether they have sex, what their ships look like, how they work, and how they have been working with governments on Earth for decades. Cannon also learned from her work with clients that almost all so-called abduction cases are actually mutual agreements between humans and ETs made before incarnating to help one another.

Cannon's five-volume series, *The Convoluted Universe*, also offers exacting details about a range of topics, including the experiences of people who were regressed to learn about lives on other planets; beings who are made entirely of energy; that reality is merely a hologram; that we are fragments of multifaceted souls, with many living in nonhuman bodies; and how much help ETs have been providing to the Earth and humanity as we move through this period of transformation and maturity.

Holt has been an educator, channeler, and author since 1985, focusing on understanding consciousness and awareness beyond human identity. For the last thirty years, she has channeled Sasha, a Pleiadian female, and Germane, a nonphysical group consciousness. She has written five books: *The Prism of Lyra*, which explores the cosmology of ET life; *Visitors from Within*, which presents the experiences of individuals who have encountered ETs; *Preparing for Contact: A Guide to Understanding and Preparing for Extraterrestrial Contact*; *Millennium: Tools for the Coming Changes*, a guidebook designed to help readers navigate profound shifts in consciousness and human evolution; and *The Golden Lake: Wisdom from the Stars for Life on Earth*, which presents a variety of topics channeled from Vega, Sirius, and the Pleiades to help humanity through its next phase of development.

Hand Clow and Clow gained popularity in the 1980s and 1990s by publishing several books on astrology and astronomy (see Chapter 5). Hand Clow was among the first to publish books based on channeled material from Satya from the Alcyone system in the Pleiades star cluster.

The following list includes other prominent channelers of nonphysical entities (links to their websites can be found in the Suggested Reading section for this chapter):

- Darryl Anka—He channels Bashar, an ET offering guidance on personal and spiritual growth.

- Lee Carroll—He channels Kryon, a being who delivers messages about spiritual evolution and human potential.

- Patricia Cori—She channels beings from the Sirian High Council and has written extensively on their teachings.

- Esther Hicks—She channels a group of entities known as Abraham, focusing on the Law of Attraction and personal empowerment.

- Geoffrey Hoppe—He channels Tobias, who shares messages about ascension and personal empowerment.

- Wendy Kennedy—She channels the Ninth Dimensional Pleiadian Collective, sharing messages about spiritual growth and universal consciousness.

- Barbara Marciniak—She is a renowned channeler of the Pleiadians, a group of ETs.

- Paul Selig—He is a channeler and author who communicates with a collective consciousness referred to as the Guides.

- Debbie Solaris—She is an ET contactee, interdimensional traveler, and galactic historian. In 2012 she had a couple of very intense out-of-body experiences during which she found herself in the interior of a huge Arcturian mothership and saw herself interacting and communicating with Arcturian and Pleiadian ETs.

- Sasha Stone—He is a visionary and channeler known for his work on human consciousness and global transformation.

Although there are clearly many sources of information about not only our galactic family but also the history and future of humans on Earth, it seems like this information is somewhat hidden from the population at large. Why all the secrecy? In the next chapter, we will look at some possible explanations.

CHAPTER THIRTEEN

SO, WHY HAVEN'T WE BEEN CONTACTED?

"When the collective consciousness on Earth has reached a mass level with compassion and a sense of Oneness, open contact will occur. In the meantime, contact will continue to take place on an individual basis."
— *A message from the Sirians,*
channeled through Jane Hernandez-Oriol

If even a fraction of the information that the channelers discussed in Chapter 12 have shared is true, and beings from advanced ET civilizations have been involved with our planet for millennia, it seems like a great injustice has been done, as they have not shared their knowledge with us. In this chapter, we will discuss several possible reasons they have kept their distance up until now.

They are not like us. Not to disparage any of the tremendous technological and social advances we have made as a species, but we might have a few more things to learn. To add some context, archaeologists estimate that the human species is approximately three hundred thousand years old.

"We don't mean this in a judgmental or negative way; we are to some degree joking a little bit. But why would we want to land in an insane asylum where all the inmates have guns?"

—*Bashar, channeled through Darryl Anka*

However, channelers interacting with ETs estimate these beings could be millions to even billions of years older than humans. ETs are capable of transcending dimensions and manipulating physical objects with their minds on an everyday basis. This means that many aspects of advanced civilizations are undoubtedly unfathomable to us, including the idea of leaving us alone.

They have a Prime Directive. I first learned about this concept from the *Star Trek* television series and movies. Every Starship captain knew they should never interfere with the natural development of an alien world, especially a less advanced civilization that had not achieved space travel or advanced technologies. Several of the ET channelers confirm that ETs generally would not interfere with the natural development of our planet unless absolutely necessary. The idea behind the Prime Directive is to respect each culture's natural evolutionary path and give them free will.

The concept of free will also emerged when I became involved with the angelic world in my book *Looking for Angels*. In the angelic realm, there are certain angels—guardian angels—with whom we contract before we incarnate. They know our plans for this life and can intervene without our permission at any time. All other angels, no matter what level, need to be asked by us to interact in our lives.

We are not ready. This aligns with the previous two ideas concerning our maturity and evolutionary path. If the age estimates of advanced civilizations are correct, at this point in time, contact would be akin to a grade school child spending time in a university setting; it would be too early for ETs to benefit from contact with us in any significant way. Furthermore, we seem to lack a solid understanding of how to coexist with one another at this point, as we continue to kill ourselves and maintain vast disparities in wealth and living conditions globally. This global incongruity and turmoil have not escaped the attention of our galactic neighbors, as sightings of unidentified anomalous phenomena have increased significantly since the first test of the atomic bomb in 1945, when we became capable of self-destruction. When we mature enough to embrace our divine nature and adopt a more unified consciousness, we will be welcomed by our galactic family.

> "We don't mean this in a judgmental or negative way; we are to some degree joking a little bit. But why would we want to land in an insane asylum where all the inmates have guns?"
> —Bashar, channeled through Darryl Anka

We are like animals in a zoo. The Zoo Hypothesis suggests that ETs might be observing us from a distance, much like we watch animals in a zoo. They may simply be observing our behaviors and development or be waiting for us to attain a certain level of technological or social development before initiating contact.

There are communication barriers. Advanced civilizations are living in higher dimensions and communicating at levels we are currently unable to detect or comprehend. As the global levels of vibration rise and we adopt higher levels of love and acceptance, we may be better able to communicate with ETs. Bashar compared this idea to gears: "A higher frequency race will operate like a fast-spinning gear and a lower frequency civilization will be like a very slowly turning gear. If you jam those two gears together too quickly, you'll strip the gears. They have to be more synchronized before you can put them together."[1]

We're not interesting enough. ETs might consider us too primitive or unremarkable to warrant contact at this stage of our development.

They're already here. Many believe that ETs are already among us and have been for ages, either in disguise or observing us covertly. They are waiting for the right time to initiate widespread communication, trade, and knowledge.

Whether you are a firm believer, on the fence, or a healthy skeptic, the next three chapters will introduce you to our galactic family and provide ways for you to interact with them if you choose.

CHAPTER FOURTEEN

OUR GALACTIC NEIGHBORHOOD

"In the galaxy, half a billion stars have Earth-like planets
going around them. So when we look at the night sky, it
makes sense that someone is looking back at us."
—*Michio Kaku*

Of all the theories of human development, the one I like best is called Systems Theory. Developed by Russian-born American psychologist Dr. Urie Bronfenbrenner, the theory's premise is that humans develop as they become aware of and interact with their environments. For example, a newborn is only aware of their primary caregiver, usually their mother, in the first weeks of life. They gradually start to perceive that other caregivers are interacting with them, maybe their father, grandmother, or siblings. As their physical senses and cognitive abilities develop, they realize they are in a home and, at times, leave this place to visit other locations, including daycare, other houses, schools, stores, parks, and other states and countries. The newborn's perimeter of awareness and understanding expands throughout their life, and they learn how to interact with the new frontiers they encounter and how they fit into these expanded settings.

"Look around you on your planet. Look at all the different forms of life and know that from the smallest to the largest, they all have cousins on other planets."

—*Joopah, channeled through Robert Shapiro*

In the same way, as humanity expands its awareness of the possibility of life beyond this planet and follows a path of rising vibration and unity, widespread and open contact with civilizations from other planets will be initiated, resulting in an exchange of knowledge, commerce, and technology.

> "Look around you on your planet. Look at all the different forms of life and know that from the smallest to the largest, they all have cousins on other planets."
> —*Joopah, channeled through Robert Shapiro*

Our Galactic Neighbors

Now, it's time to get to know a few of our neighbors. Most of the information we have about our galactic brothers and sisters has been obtained through channeled sources. When considering content about the Star Nations, I approach each source cautiously, relying on the work of experienced channelers and seeking consensus. Among these sources, there are variations, conflicting information, and disparate interpretations—similar to the many sacred texts of the world's religions. What follows is a summary of information derived from several reputable and mature sources that have offered consistent content over many years.

STARSEEDS

We all come from somewhere. Just as many people like to trace their earthly lineage through their DNA to see which part of the world their ancestors came from, we can track our soul's journey through space and time to better understand Who we are and where our soul has led us.

As we first emerge as souls from God/Source, we may start our journey incarnating in specific civilizations throughout the universe. We may be drawn to one civilization and reincarnate multiple times on planets that the group inhabits. Over lifetimes, that civilization's unique characteristics, strengths, and gifts will become a part of Who we are, and we will emulate those characteristics effortlessly and naturally.

When someone with a long history in another galactic civilization decides to, or is asked to, come to Earth, they are referred to as a starseed. Many starseeds have incarnated here, bringing their unique talents and gifts to help in our transition.

You may be a starseed who came to Earth specifically to help. Perhaps that is why you were drawn to this book and continued reading to this chapter. As you read through the descriptions of a few of our many galactic neighbors—our brothers and sisters—one or two of them may ring true to you, and you will become aware of Who you really are and what you are here to do.

Humans like to describe ourselves through labels—European or American, Democrat or Republican, Gen Z or Gen X, Gemini or Aries. A starseed also has traits that emanate from the planetary culture from which they came. The traits presented for any starseed will vary in intensity and appear to overlap with others. In addition, just as it is difficult to precisely describe what a person from Germany or a Sagittarius is like, it is impossible to define a starseed solely based on their origins. After all, the advanced planetary civilizations are hundreds of millions of years old and have had their own evolutionary paths. In addition, many of us are a blend of several galactic civilizations, as we may have incarnated on several planets over our soul's journey.

Whatever the reason that you have been drawn to the idea of starseeds and are interested in uncovering your galactic lineage by learning about our celestial brothers and sisters, you will also learn more about yourself.

THE LYRANS

We will begin our galactic investigation with the Lyra constellation, located approximately 652 light-years from Earth. Vega is the brightest star in this constellation (located much closer to us than the rest of the constellation, at twenty-five light-years) and can be seen without a telescope in the Northern Hemisphere's night sky during the summer months. Astronomers have identified multiple planets in the Lyran system, some of which could be habitable.

Starting our discussion with Lyra makes sense because it is one of the oldest constellations and, according to several sources, the place where human consciousness began.[1,2,3] The Lyrans are the oldest galactic civilization in the universe, with a heritage of wisdom, love, and service to others that spans hundreds of millions or even billions of years.

The Lyrans began their journey when God/Source decided to split in order to create a different version of itself. While there are a few variations of the story of their evolutionary journey, the consensus is that they flourished on Avalon and other neighboring planets within the Lyra constellation for millions of years—until an unfortunate event happened. Inhabitants from a neighboring star system, Draco (where the Reptilians originated), invaded their star system and massacred millions of Lyrans. The Draconians were dark and of service only to themselves, and they easily overran their peaceful and trusting neighbors. While the Lyrans were not warriors, they were capable of space travel. They fled to several star systems—including Andromeda, the Pleiades, Orion, and Sirius—eventually influencing the development of life on Earth. Some believe that Lyrans are the core race of all humanoid civilizations in our galaxy.

The Lyrans' primary form has a blend of humanoid and feline features, including feline-like eyes and pointed ears. Although there are many variations of this form, which have evolved over millions of years, their humanoid features are likely more prominent than the feline. Their subtle, elegant, catlike ways convey the wisdom, deep understanding, and higher states of consciousness attributed to feline energy.

Because the Lyrans established themselves across dozens of star systems, many interplanetary species contain Lyran characteristics. In addition, the destruction of the Lyrans' home planet, forcing them to flee to other worlds, significantly impacted their physical and cultural development. In general, you may have Lyran traits if you are

- An old soul,

- A natural leader,

- Drawn to the stars,

- Independent,

- Quietly confident,

- A problem solver,

- Eager for exploration, or

- Trustworthy.

THE VEGANS

The Vegan civilization is also in the Lyra constellation and is associated with the star Vega. Although no planet has been identified with this star, in 2021 the American

Museum of Natural History reported that astronomers had found a type of giant planet similar to Uranus or Neptune orbiting close to the star, possibly a planet like a "hot Jupiter," physically similar to Jupiter but with a very short orbit.[4]

Vegans are considered one of the first civilizations to develop and use space travel to colonize other star systems. However, they are not known to be warlike conquerors; instead, they brought spiritual wisdom, creativity, and advanced intelligence to their inhabited worlds. Reports of what Vegans look like vary; some describe Vegans as having blue or lavender skin and white or silver hair, while others suggest they can take on humanoid forms, with dark complexions and black hair and eyes.

Lyssa Royal Holt provided a fascinating depiction of the Vegan demeanor in her book *The Prism of Lyra: An Exploration of Human Galactic Heritage*. She likened this species to the Vulcans in the television series *Star Trek*.[5] In this sci-fi show, the Vulcans almost destroyed themselves and their planet through several wars. At the brink of destruction, they collectively decided that emotion was at the root of their problems and removed all emotion, relying only on logic to survive. Holt stated that, like the fictional Vulcans, Vegans ultimately destroyed themselves by engineering themselves to have no emotion. Vegans do not exist as they did millennia ago, yet their ideology lives on and is embedded within other cultures.

In general, you may have Vegan traits if you are
- Wise and intuitive;

- Intelligent and like to learn;

- Driven to raise humanity's consciousness and promote peace;

- Artistic, often excelling in music and the arts;

- Passionate about spiritual expression;

- Highly empathetic;

- Deeply connected to nature; or

- Psychic (clairaudience and telepathy).

THE PLEIADEANS

I was first drawn to the Pleiades star cluster as a child, fascinated by the stories of the Bible, particularly those in the Old Testament. I was also an avid astronomer, aware of many celestial bodies in the night sky. In the story of Job, he began to complain as God was testing him, and God's response caught my attention: "Can you bind the chains of the Pleiades or loosen the belt of Orion?" (Job 38:31).

That rhetorical question was meant to show Job that God's plans and purposes are far greater than humans can perceive, but it made me wonder why those star clusters were explicitly mentioned. After some research, I discovered that Orion and the Pleiades are special because all their stars travel in the same direction at the same speed. This means that they look the same over thousands of years, as compared to clusters like the Big Dipper, which change over time because their stars are on different trajectories. This impressed me because it validated that whoever wrote the book of Job thousands of years ago knew that the Pleiades and Orion would remain unchanged.

The Pleiades star cluster is located in the constellation of Taurus, approximately 440 light-years away, and visible in the fall and winter in the Northern Hemisphere. Several sources agree that the Pleiadians are closely related to the

Lyrans because they settled in the Pleiades after they were scattered across the galaxies looking for new places to live. Holt (channeling Sasha) added that the Lyrans who traveled to the Pleiades landed first on Earth. However, after several generations, they found it difficult to adapt to Earth's physical and electromagnetic environment. In an attempt to correct the issue, they intermingled their genetic structures with those of Earth's primates. Their efforts worked, more Lyrans arrived on Earth, and a faction of the Earthlings/Lyrans wanted to move on. This group headed to the seven stars of the Pleiadian system and created a stable culture that lasted for thousands of years.

Possibly due to their shared human genetics from the Lyran migrants, Pleiadians appear similar to Scandinavians. They are usually described as tall, physically attractive, and youthful, regardless of their age. Some say they live primarily in the upper-level dimensions. As a result, they are generally peaceful, benevolent, ethical, and interested in Earth's future from an environmental and sociological perspective.

In general, you may have Pleiadian traits if you

- Are driven to help heal and uplift humanity,

- Are a visionary or dreamer,

- Have a sense of a deep purpose,

- Have a strong connection to healing,

- Have a strong aversion to harm and violence,

- Are highly intuitive,

- Are good with animals, or

- Feel like an outsider.

The Zetas, often
called the Grays, ...
have been depicted
as emotionless and
focused on abductions
and memory-
erasing scientific
experiments, but
those who know them
well say that these
characterizations
are untrue.

THE SIRIANS

The Sirius star system includes two stars: Sirius A and Sirius B. Sirius A is about 25 times brighter than the sun and is located about 8.6 light-years from Earth. Due to its intrinsic luminosity and proximity to our solar system, Sirius A is the brightest star visible from Earth. Sirius B is a white dwarf star that is much smaller and less luminous than Sirius A and orbits around its larger counterpart. The two stars are a part of the constellation Canis Major, often called the "Dog Star" due to its association with the Great Dog in mythology.

Some say that the Pleiadians and Sirians have been the ETs most involved with our planet in recent times. As discussed in Chapter 12, the temples of Malta were designed so that Sirius would pass all the entrances of all the temples at some point in time. Sirius also aligns with the Queen's Chamber in the Great Pyramid of Egypt. In addition, the Dogon tribe of Africa has a historical connection to Sirius. Surprisingly, artifacts and drawings handed down through generations of the Dogon people describe Sirius B's elliptical journey around Sirius A with an accuracy that predates modern telescopes. The Dogon attribute this wisdom to teachings from Sirian ETs.

Sirians typically present as short beings, around four feet tall, with smooth gray skin, elongated black eyes, and elongated heads. They are known for their seriousness, focus, and highly intelligent nature. Sirians maintain a mindset of constant improvement and discovery.

In general, you may have Sirian traits if you

- Have a vivid imagination,

- Are intuitive,

- Prefer the company of smaller groups,

- Find trust to be hard-earned,

- Are shy and reserved,

- Prefer the road less traveled,

- Have a focus on unfinished business, or

- Care deeply about protecting nature.

THE ZETAS OR GRAYS

Zeta Reticuli is a binary star system located in the southern constellation Reticulum, approximately 39.3 light-years from Earth. The system has two sunlike stars: Zeta 1 Reticuli and Zeta 2 Reticuli. They are most visible from the Southern Hemisphere, particularly during January.

The Zetas, often called the Grays, are among popular culture's most iconic alien archetypes. Unfortunately, because they are less capable of expressing a wide range of emotions than we are, they have been depicted as emotionless and focused on abductions and memory-erasing scientific experiments, but those who know them well say that these characterizations are untrue.

The Grays present themselves as small and slender humanoid beings with smooth gray skin; large, almond-shaped black eyes; and elongated heads with no external features like ears or noses. They appear to be exclusively telepathic and not capable of producing oral language. In explaining how different species migrated and evolved throughout time, Holt stated that the Vegan race was the genetic source of the Grays and that Vegans eventually became the Zetas.

Author Robert Shapiro has been channeling entities from various dimensions, timelines, and realms for more than thirty years. In his 724-page book, *The Zetas:*

History, Hybrids, and Human Contacts, he provided extensive and detailed information on what these beings are like, their mission, and several documented encounters with Earthlings. He described them as future versions of humanity, millions of years ahead in evolution. According to Shapiro's channeling, the Zetas are highly intellectual and scientific, and they are fascinated by humans because they view us as their past selves.[6]

In general, you may have Zeta traits if you

- Help make other humans aware of other intelligences, beings, and races;

- Focus on service to others;

- Have intellectual curiosity;

- Have deep empathy;

- Have a sense of purpose;

- Have memories and dreams of ET contact;

- Exhibit advanced problem-solving skills; or

- Are highly introspective.

We focused on the Lyrans, Vegans, Pleiadians, Sirians, and Grays because these five galactic civilizations provide examples of different types of planetary civilizations, their developmental history, and how their traits may show up in human starseeds. But these are only a few of the many civilizations that exist outside of our solar system. The following are some other civilizations that you may be drawn to:

- **Andromedans**—These beings are from the Andromeda Galaxy, about 2.5 million light-years from Earth. They teach us that the nature of consciousness is to be fluid.

- **Arcturians**—This nonphysical civilization is located in the Arcturus star system, part of the constellation Boötes, approximately 36.7 light-years away from Earth. Arcturans are deeply connected to Earth and have played a significant role in its development since the planet's inception.

- **Reptilians**—Many Reptilian beings exist in our galactic family, but few are hostile. They help us address the processed and denied fears within us.

- **Insectoids**—Many Insectoid species have been in contact with Earth for thousands of years. Their societies are based on the idea of a group thinking.

- **Orions**—Many souls from Orion have come to Earth to help us heal our polarizing attitudes, beliefs, and behaviors.

- **Essassani**—These beings are human/Zeta hybrids; they are a highly evolved species that will assist Earth in our transition.

Their Journey Is Our Journey

While it is interesting to try to identify our galactic lineage, there is a far more important reason to understand the history of the Star Nations. The motivation for ET involvement in our planet is to help us grow through the developmental paths that they have encountered over millions of years. Learning about their journey can help us enormously by guiding us on a positive path, avoiding the same mistakes they made, preventing us from destroying ourselves, and when we are ready, helping us directly with knowledge and technology, interstellar commerce, and navigating our new-found universe.

The Galactic Heritage Card deck developed by Holt, Sasha, and Germane is an excellent way to discover the lessons learned from our rich heritage and to glean personal insights. A description of this deck is included at the end of this chapter.

Governance

Learning about the various planets and civilizations and how they interact with one another—most of the time in peaceful ways, but in rare cases in brutal wars—brings to mind an important question: Is there a governing body or group that manages, leads, guides, or protects the thousands or millions of diverse civilizations in the universe?

The answer, according to many channelers who have regularly interacted with ETs for many years, is yes. The most common group mentioned is the Galactic Federation; other groups, which may be governing bodies focused on specific areas or subgroups of larger governing bodies, include the Galactic Federation of Light, Intergalactic Federation, Council of Light, Council of Nine, Alliance of Light, Galactic Senate, and Association of Worlds.

The Galactic Federation received attention in 2020, when Haim Eshed, former head of the Israeli Defense Ministry's space directorate stated in an interview with Israel's *Yedioth ahronoth* newspaper that agreements had been made between species through the Galactic Federation: "There is an agreement between the United States government and the aliens. They signed a contract with us to do experiments here."[7] Several of Dolores Cannon's subjects also described agreements between the US government and other countries and

ETs that allowed them access to a material commonly found on Earth in exchange for information about new technologies. It is important to remember that all information about galactic governance is obtained through channeled sources, with the exception of Eshed's interview.

There are few similarities between interplanetary governing groups and any governmental body on our planet. Our default is to compare galactic governance to how our country manages its population and interacts with other countries. We are steeped in our third-dimension reality, and with that comes separation, polarity, and a strong "us vs them" mentality. Projecting our experiences and beliefs onto the management of other civilizations is unrealistic. We have much to learn about how the universe works, how it's managed, and what our place in it is—and we will learn, over time.

While information about what exactly the Galactic Federation is, who its members are, whether they are a part of a larger group, and how they interact with Earth is hard to find, several channelers agree about how the Galactic Federation and its equivalents govern our universe. The following explanation is a compilation of how Darryl Anka, Cannon, Barbara Hand Clow, Holt, and others describe what the Galactic Federation is and does and how interplanetary interactions are managed. When we become a part of the federation, more information about its structure will be conveyed to us.

The Galactic Federation and its counterpart groups comprise advanced beings centered in light and love, numbering in the hundreds of thousands or even millions, from a multitude of galaxies and planets. The group functions as a collective network in which there is no hierarchy of power. It is currently observing our evolutionary process, and eventually we will be able to become a part of the federation and initiate trade, commerce, and knowledge exchange with other civilizations.

The federation assists humanity in navigating challenges and awakening to a higher state of awareness and interconnectedness with the cosmos, manifesting unity and peace on Earth. It helps us to dissolve the paradigm of materialism, ego, and separation, leading to a spiritual awakening and recognition of a higher consciousness. Its intention is not to "save" us or other civilizations, but rather to empower us to make our own choices and evolve at our own pace.

How specifically do the federation and other governing bodies interact with Earth to do all these wonderful things? The answer is that we do not know for sure. To what extent have ETs been involved with our development? What can they do? What can't they do? Who decides? We can speculate that these questions all relate back to the interplanetary governing body or bodies involved with Earth.

When questioning the extent of ET involvement on Earth, remember that whatever happens aligns with our awakening higher state of awareness and interconnectedness with the cosmos. It manifests unity and peace on Earth and always maintains our free will and choices. Some authors suggest that ETs are only allowed to intervene if necessary to avoid catastrophic harm to us. As parents, sometimes we teach our children, and sometimes they need to learn from their own mistakes. However, we can't let them unknowingly harm themselves. The same may be true of ET involvement with humans.

What about Bad Guys?

While several channelers agree that there are "bad actors" in the universe, they also agree that the vast majority of all galactic civilizations are benevolent and focused on love and light, with very few having malevolent intentions. An interesting common designation to describe the overall demeanor of civilizations is if they are in service to self or in service to others.

As mentioned earlier in this chapter, significant conflicts among galactic civilizations have been reported. For example, the Draconians invaded Lyra, resulting in the deaths of millions of Lyrans. Some suggest this event led to the formation of the Galactic Federation. Other conflicts include the battles in the Orion constellation between the Draconians, Orionians, and Galactic Federation. A friend told me that recently the Galactic Federation easily thwarted an attempt by a nefarious group that was planning to invade our solar system. Obviously, these reports are impossible to verify, as they come from channeled sources. However, after we achieve contact, we may be able to get answers to these types of questions.

While almost all our galactic neighbors act in service to others and have the highest intentions for us, not all of the universe is love and light. Thus, the question of how we can ensure that we have a positive experience when contacting ETs inevitably arises. This is discussed in detail in Chapters 15 and 16.

On a final note on the subject of good and bad Star Nations, there is a philosophical component to consider. This is the idea that there needs to be bad to define good and that neither could exist without the other. It is outside the scope of this book to delve into this topic, but the works of many prominent philosophers like Friedrich Nietzsche, St. Augustine, and Thomas Aquinas are good places to start. Additionally, there is a practical perspective to consider as well. This relates to the question, Are all things that seem bad, really bad? For example, if the Draconians did not invade Lyra, the Lyrans would not have spread their civilization across the universe. It seems a bit of a stretch, but another example is if Judas had not betrayed Christ, would Christianity have spread as broadly as it has? There are other examples like this, and they pose interesting scenarios to think about.

Experiential Exercise: Galactic Heritage Cards

During the first ten years that Holt was channeling Sasha and Germane, she sought to create a card system that would that would enable seekers to not only identify their galactic heritage but also understand the karmic influences impacting their lives in real time. In 2010 she and Germane developed a 108-card deck to do just that. The Galactic Heritage Deck is similar to a tarot card deck in that it has images with references to archetypal themes that can help us identify lessons we are learning. The deck addresses the divine and universal journey that all beings go through—from unity to polarity and back to unity—by referencing how our galactic forefathers experienced this process and applying lessons they learned to our planet.

I have been learning to use this deck on myself over the last few months and have been amazed by the messages and guidance that have come through. Maybe someday I will use it to help others.

CHAPTER FIFTEEN

PREPARING FOR CONTACT

"As the world progresses toward a global civilization and an organic unity, the potential for a sustained and open relationship between humans and extraterrestrial visitors will increase. It is our responsibility as humans to similarly prepare ourselves mentally, physically, and spiritually for the next step in our relationship with these visitors."
—*Steven M. Greer, MD, International Director of Center for the Study of Extraterrestrial Intelligence*

The following two chapters will help you understand that robust communication with ETs is a two-way street between them and us, and there is no "magic bullet" of connection that will work every time with everyone. We must remember that nonphysical beings live outside our three-dimensional reality, at higher vibrational levels. They must take action to slow their vibrational levels so they can interact with us. There are several things we can do to help make contact easier for both us and them, but first it is helpful to understand the various levels of contact.

Contact experiences
are not just external;
the most important
connection in
initiating interaction
with ETs starts
within ourselves.

Close Encounters Classification System

J. Allen Hynek, PhD, was an astronomer and scientific advisor to the US Air Force UFO Investigations (Project Sign, Project Grudge, and Project Blue Book).[1] Initially skeptical of unidentified flying objects (UFOs), now referred to as unidentified anomalous phenomena (UAPs), he became convinced that ET sightings were worthy of study. He also consulted on one of Steven Spielberg's movies about ET contact, inspiring its title, *Close Encounters of the Third Kind*. Dr. Hynek developed the first three levels of contact.[2]

> **First Kind:** A UAP is seen but leaves no physical evidence.
>
> **Second Kind:** A UAP is seen and there are associated phenomena, such as physical evidence, electronic equipment interference, ground burn marks, or physical marks or effects on witnesses.
>
> **Third Kind:** An entity or entities is observed near a UAP.

Argentine parapsychologist and UAP researcher Fabio Zerpa contributed significantly to ET research by reporting on more than three thousand sightings and possible ET contacts. In 1977 Zerpa identified the fourth and fifth levels of contact, also known as the Zerpa Classification.[3]

> **Fourth Kind:** A so-called alien abduction, in which a human is taken from their physical location, takes place. Some interpretations expand this idea to include situations when a person is not moved to a ship but is detained in some way.
>
> **Fifth Kind:** Direct communication between humans and ETs—through audible, telepathic, mental, or other conscious communication—takes place.

Other researchers have suggested two additional kinds of encounters.[4]

> **Sixth Kind:** A UAP-related event that results in injury or death takes place.
>
> **Seventh Kind:** Human-alien hybridization occurs. Numerous examples of the seventh kind—occurring on Earth and on many planets in our galactic past—can be found in Dolores Cannon's and Lyssa Royal Holt's work.

It's easy to find examples of most of these encounters in television shows, podcasts, social media, and books that describe first-hand sightings, strange markings, and reports of communication with ETs, with some being more credible than others. The kinds of encounters we experience depend on several factors, such as prior contracts with ETs before this lifetime, exceptional circumstances in which ET involvement is deemed necessary for the sake of the planet, and our efforts to be respectfully and responsibly open to communication in order to benefit life on Earth.

It Starts with Us

The biggest obstacle to connecting with ETs and other non-physical beings is the assumption that we don't need to take any action—that the responsibility lies solely with them to reach out to us. While there are countless reports of individuals simply going about their daily lives and unexpectedly experiencing a supernatural event with an ET, such events are relatively rare, but growing in number.

The idea that we need to focus on ourselves first to establish a connection with ETs seems counterintuitive, but it is critical. Ricardo González Corpancho, a well-known ufologist, contactee, and author from Lima, Peru, explains that contact experiences are not just external; the most important connection in initiating interaction with ETs starts within ourselves.[5] Many authors and sources offer ways to prepare for contact. We will review a few critical components of contact in this chapter and present a detailed protocol in the next chapter.

PHYSICAL PREPARATION

As mentioned earlier, our minds reside partly in our bodies, specifically in our brain and nervous system. As we all know, a healthy body helps maintain a healthy mind. In preparing to connect with ETs, physical health is a significant factor and cannot be ignored. As you will see in the approaches to prepare for contact, as well as the protocol provided in the next chapter, maintaining a healthy lifestyle in terms of diet and exercise, along with a stable emotional and spiritual life, will help prepare you for contact.

Brain Wave Awareness

As you know, our brains register inputs from the outside physical world, in addition to memory, to help us create our perceived reality. In processing this information, our brain's processing speed changes, which correlates with different waking and sleeping states. Understanding the different brain wave frequencies and how they impact our perception of the world is a key component in preparing for contact with ETs.

As we go through our daily lives at work, play, and interacting with others, our brains are operating in the beta frequencies, which range from 12 to 30 cycles per second (Hz). When we are somewhat concentrating on what we are doing—such as when driving, performing mundane activities, or daydreaming—our brains slow down to the alpha frequencies, ranging from 8 to 12 Hz. During the time right before we fall asleep or just after we begin to wake up, our brains are producing theta frequencies at 4–8 Hz. In her books, Holt, channeling Sasha from the Pleiades, stated that the theta frequency, experienced as light sleep, is the most common way ETs communicate with us. In states of deep sleep, at .5–4 Hz (delta frequencies), we are unconscious and unaware of our conscious mind. According to Sasha, channeled by Holt:

> If we were to tell you that contact experiences are most likely to occur in a particular brain wave state, it would be theta. Theta and delta are separated enough from the conscious mind that you may or may not remember the encounters you have when your brain has switched to that frequency.[6]

We can train ourselves to move in and out of the theta frequencies with practice (see the experiential exercise at the end of this chapter). However, it is beneficial to first understand how our brain frequencies influence our waking states.

Cognitive Preparation

There are a few areas of cognitive preparation that we can undertake to ready ourselves for contact. The most critical area, by far, is understanding how our conscious perception of ourselves is compartmentalized and how to move beyond that.

While it seems complex, we can learn to decompartmentalize our consciousness over time, and when we do, it will transform our lives. This idea comes to us through Sasha from the Pleiades, as channeled by Holt and recounted in her book *Preparing for Contact.*[7] Holt presented this concept with an analogy: You are in a lecture hall listening to a speaker. Assume that their head represents their conscious mind or ego, the area from their neck to their hips represents their subconscious mind, and the area from their hips to their feet represents their unconscious mind. When listening to the speaker from the back of the room, you assume that all communication is coming from their head; you do not notice that their hands are gesturing or that they are standing in a particular way. You are missing out on many of the speaker's nonverbal cues.

In this analogy, our minds are separated into three levels: the awakened state of the ego (head), an intermittent state of awareness of our subconscious (torso), and our unconscious or the deep-seated thoughts and feelings that we are unaware of (legs). In our current state of evolution, the three parts do not communicate with one another naturally or consistently.

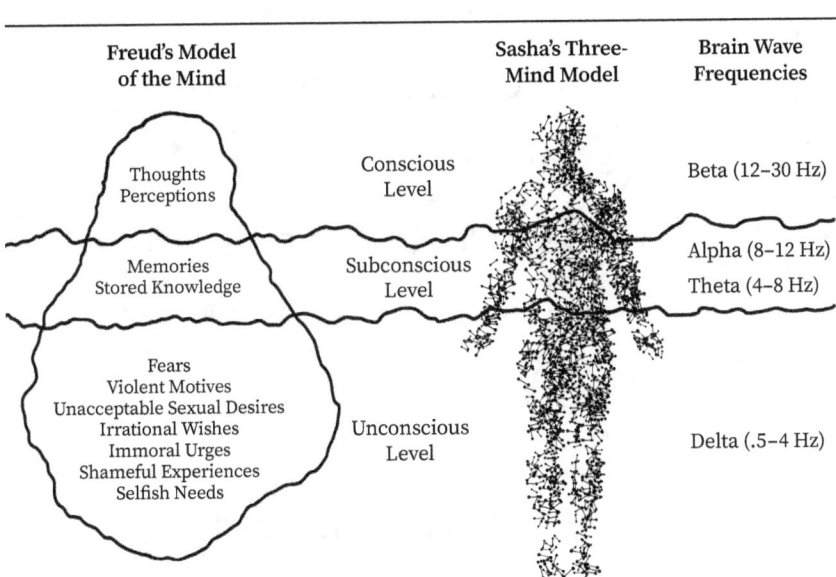

ETs see all three levels of the mind at the same time.

Figure 7. A comparison of Sigmund Freud's model of the mind and Sasha's three-mind model, channeled through Lyssa Royal Holt.

"All people who have
any type of contact
on a more physical
basis have been
prepared telepathically
beforehand. This
preparation occurs
either in the dream
state, meditation, or
it is directly given to
the subconscious or
unconscious mind."

— *Sasha, channeled
through Lyssa Royal Holt*

Interestingly, this model aligns with Sigmund Freud's structure of the mind, which he compared to the three parts of an iceberg. In Freud's model, our conscious mind is the part of the iceberg above the water, but the bulk of our mind, the subconscious and unconscious parts, is below the water. One difference between the two models is that Freud provided more detailed information about the contents of the unconscious mind than Sasha. Freud described the unconscious mind as containing all the fears that we are not aware of, in addition to selfish and primal urges of violence, unacceptable sexual desires, and shame. Sasha's model centers on fears, which can be of anything, however irrational they may seem (see Figure 7).

One fundamental difference between ETs and humans is that ETs perceive all three levels of the mind simultaneously. In contrast, we compartmentalize our consciousness and are almost entirely aware of one level: the conscious mind. According to Sasha, our fears block our energy and frequency, preventing an integrated self and creating disharmony. Freud explained that the fears and base urges of the unconscious mind bubble up through the subconscious and can manifest in dreams, as well as shaping many aspects of our personalities in ways we are not consciously aware of.

If left unprocessed, fears manifest as cognitive and emotional turmoil, preventing a true understanding of ourselves, higher levels of awareness, and ET connections. It is difficult for ETs to connect with us through our disorganized, compartmentalized minds, so they are forced to communicate with us in whatever way they can, usually on a subconscious level. When we wonder why we do not have more open communication with ETs, most of the time it is because we are focused just on our conscious awareness and discounting our dreams as not being real. ETs may have been communicating with you for years at the subconscious levels through dreams, insights, synchronicities, signs, and symbols, but we dismiss these communications as meaningless. Interestingly, Sasha further specified, "All people who have any type of contact on a more physical basis have been prepared telepathically beforehand. This preparation occurs either in the dream state, meditation, or it is directly given to the subconscious or unconscious mind."[8]

EMOTIONAL PREPARATION: EMBRACING OUR SHADOW SELVES

With a few exceptions, ET contact can only occur once we fully embrace ourselves on both conscious and unconscious levels to the extent that we are aware, and reconcile with our shadow selves. It is interesting that working with and accepting our shadow self is not only critical in developing unity consciousness, as mentioned in Chapter 9, but also a key factor in establishing ET contact.

Our shadow self is the things we do and the desires or emotions we feel that we believe are socially unacceptable, immoral, or uncomfortable, or conflict with how we would like to see ourselves and how we want others to see us. According to psychologist Carl Jung, the shadow personifies everything that a person refuses to acknowledge about themselves and yet is always thrusting itself upon them directly or indirectly.[9]

Jung's concept of the shadow self is described as "clouding the mind"—but from within. What we refuse to see in ourselves (anger, desire, shame) often emerges unconsciously and becomes the force that controls us. For those of you who are familiar with the dramatic radio shows of the 1930s, the Mutual Broadcasting System produced a show from 1937 to 1954 called *The Shadow* that brought this idea to life. The main character, Lamont Cranston, used his psychic abilities to "cloud" the minds of criminals and other dark forces of society to bring them to justice.

> "Who knows what evil lurks in the hearts of men? The Shadow knows. ... Mwah-ha-ha."
> —The Shadow

It is important to know that the shadow self does not always refer to negative characteristics or behaviors. For example, if a person is told their entire life they should keep quiet and not share their thoughts, their shadow self will consist of the urges to be more assertive and make their voice known. If a person believes that homosexuality is immoral and they become very angry when the topic comes up in conversation, yet they are attracted to others of the same sex, they will struggle with their "immoral" attractions until they resolve the conflict by accepting themselves as they are.

Understanding your shadow self will require some effort. You cannot simply think about it for a few days, come up with a list, and then move on. Real shadow work is being open to exploring unacceptable parts of you that are deeply buried in your subconscious and unconscious mind, and unrecognizable to you. It can be upsetting to discover feelings and attitudes that go beyond what you know about your deepest fears. Not addressing this part of ourselves may be why most humans have unconscious resistance to ET contact.

Sasha made the following suggestions to help us unlock our deep-seated fears and find common ground with ETs:[10]

- Work on dissolving your fears.

- Become aware of the rigid views of reality that you hold (you may not even be conscious of some).

- Begin to know who you are and begin to consciously change perceptions of the reality you have outgrown.

- Begin replacing these perceptions with new and more expansive points of view.

- Go within, as deeply as you can. Find your own demons.

- Find your own fears.

- Find the part of you that hates yourself.

- Find that part of you that is not you but merely a reflection of your programming from this life and other lives.

- Accept and embrace all parts of yourself.

A common misconception is that we must be perfect in every way to connect. Sasha pointed out that we don't have to remove our darker characteristics but befriend them. It is not easy to look into the mirror of our soul and see all that is there—the good and the bad, the light and the love, and the ugliness. When we can accept and befriend all our parts, we have reached our unconscious mind and begun the integration process, and we will see things begin to happen in our lives. Many people have done this through techniques such as rebirthing, regression, dream work, or rituals, which can lead to profound changes and initiate relationships with our galactic families.

Experiential Exercise: Shadow Work

An excellent introduction to shadow work and how we can begin our work with it can be found in the article "100+ Deep Shadow Work Prompts to Accept Yourself and Move Forward" by Rosey LaVine.[11]

NOTE: Exploring the shadow self may stir deep emotional discomfort. If you experience distress, please seek support from a qualified mental health professional.

Guidance for Positive Experiences

Some people believe that contact with any ET is positive. Dr. Steven Greer, a prominent ufologist who founded the Center for the Study of Extraterrestrial Intelligence and the Disclosure Project in order to promote peaceful contact with ETs, teaches that all contact with ET civilizations is peaceful and nonhostile, and that fear-based narratives are part of disinformation campaigns. He reasons that all ET civilizations that have attained interstellar technologies are benevolent.[12,13,14] However, despite the research he has completed and the effective contact methods he has developed, his opinion that all ET contact is positive is not shared by other seasoned ET channelers.

Several of the channelers presented throughout this book have provided guidance on how to connect with ETs. They all emphasize that preparation, intention, and discernment are critical parts in our plans to contact ETs. Figure 8 outlines four of these channelers' thoughts on how best to approach contact.

CHANNELER	SAFETY EMPHASIS	ADVICE
Barbara Marciniak	Energetic discernment	Clear your emotional baggage and raise your frequency. Not all ETs are benevolent; fear attracts manipulation. Trust your intuition; love repels interference.[15,16]
Lyssa Royal Holt	Inner maturity and vibrational alignment	Safe contact begins with inner work—integrate your shadow self. Your contact will mirror your inner state. Approach ETs with curiosity.[17,18]
Jane Roberts (Seth)	Belief-driven reality	Your beliefs shape your reality. Avoid fear-based expectations, which can manifest undesirable experiences, including psychic interference.[19,20,21]
Darryl Anka (Bashar)	Vibrational resonance and excitement	Align with joy and excitement. Fear-based contact scenarios are reflections of internal discord. Benevolent ETs will only engage with humans who are vibrationally ready.[22,23]

Figure 8. Advice from channelers for positive experiences.

WE ARE SOVEREIGN BEINGS

As we embrace Who we really are, we learn that we are a part of God/Source just like every other living being. This means that you have the ability to discern any experience with an ET and set energetic boundaries. All you have to do is ask, out loud if you need to, whomever you are most connected with—a specific deity, archangel, guardian angel, ascended master, or ET—if you wish to stop or change what is happening.

Holt presents a balanced approach to contact by warning that frightened or ungrounded individuals may attract lower-vibration beings. She stresses the importance of confronting inner fears to avoid projecting them onto ETs. In her book *Preparing for Contact*, she wrote:

> No ET with any negative intention is going to show up and cause problems. This isn't because we keep them out; it is because we've created a specific energy field. Only those of like vibration can even perceive what is going on here. If there is anyone with any ill intention, they don't even see you.[24]

Practical Safety Tips
PREPARING

- Educate yourself using the resources mentioned in this book about preparing for contact, including addressing your shadow self and establishing habits to raise your vibrational levels.

- Remember that our default reality is the physical world and our waking state and that most ET contact takes place at the subconscious and unconscious levels, especially prior to physical contact. Keep your expectations to a minimum, and above all, keep your mind open to whatever happens.

- Review the protocols for preparing for contact in the next chapter, Corpancho's videos, and Holt's book *Preparing for Contact*. Decide which protocol you would like to try.

- As you learn more about other Star Nations, you will find that many other civilizations do not have the emotional range of humans. For example, the Zetas almost extinguished themselves by removing emotion from their psyche because they saw that emotions caused a host of problems. Over time, they learned to appreciate the value of emotions and are slowly incorporating them back into their lives. In the meantime, their behavior during direct physical contact with humans can appear to be emotionless and robotic. During their visit, they are doing their job and that's it. You can see why it can upset people when, in the midst of a shocking experience, the ETs show no signs of emotion.

CONTACTING

- Let at least one person know what you are doing. If possible, connect with someone familiar with ET contact. Greer's CE5 Contact app includes an option to locate like-minded people near you to connect with. When connecting with others you do not know, set some time to get to know them via a phone call or at a restaurant. Tap into your intuition when meeting with them. It's a crazy world out there.

- Use breath work or guided meditations to center yourself before contact attempts.

- Use whatever protocol you would like to try. Remember that establishing contact takes practice, so give it some time, maybe weeks or months; be ready to go through multiple attempts; and change your protocols as you wish.

DISCERNMENT DURING THE EXPERIENCE

- Ask yourself, Does this feel positive and light, or dark and negative? Is this aligned with love?

- Notice sensations like tightness, warmth, or tingling when engaging with a presence or message.

- Set energetic boundaries before and during any contact. Don't forget you have a spirit team of angels, spirits, and ETs that can alleviate any concerns you may have.

AFTER YOUR SESSION

- Write down everything—images, emotions, phrases— without filtering. This way you can track your experiences over time.

- Be thankful for whatever happened or didn't happen, knowing that you have astute guides with you on your journey.

A HEALING PROCESS

The center of the cognitive and emotional preparation process is healing. In the three-part model of the mind described above, it takes many people decades to learn to accept themselves at a conscious level. Delving into the subconscious and unconscious levels of the mind can be disturbing for anyone. The only solution to effectively address this discomfort is by applying unconditional love to ourselves and embracing our true divine nature, with pure love at our core. This, as Corpancho stated, is most critical in preparing for interactions with ETs.

The more we prepare our body, mind, and emotions for contact with ETs, the more likely we are to have meaningful interactions. One very effective way to fast-track your self-acceptance and self-love is to stand in front of a mirror and steadily gaze into your eyes, slowly repeating the words, "I love you." You may have a tendency to look away from yourself, but with practice and by setting positive intentions, you can deepen your love for yourself and others.

Protocols

When you are ready, you can begin to think about taking action to reach out and establish contact with a specific ET. Remember, while physical contact is quite dramatic and impactful, most contact experiences occur at the subconscious and unconscious levels and may already be happening with you. Numerous protocols are available to help facilitate a connection; one protocol is provided in the next chapter. However, there is much more to making a connection than going through a to-do list. There is no magic trick or game to summon ETs at our whim; they have their responsibilities and tasks, and as advanced beings, they are the ones who set the agenda for encounters in our three-dimensional lives.

The first step in a contact protocol, as both Corpancho and Sasha suggested, is the connection within yourself. I recommend viewing Corpancho's video "Portals and Protocols of ET Contact." In it, Corpancho explained that, beyond our internal preparation, there are different protocols for different types of encounters.[25] For example, the protocols for seeing lights, telepathic communication, projection into other realities, or engaging in dimensional realities all vary to some extent. He stressed the importance of a good diet and rest before any intense encounter.

He also stated that whatever preparation you do or whatever protocol you use, if you do not have good intentions, nothing will happen.

Experiential Exercises: Creating a Theta State

Being aware of contact with ETs and other beings like angels and passed loved ones on the subconscious and unconscious levels can be just as profound as seeing a ship, seeing lights, or other physical experiences. As mentioned, these experiences mostly happen during the theta state, which occurs during light sleep and meditation. When you accept the idea that many experiences during these states are real, your life can change significantly. This is because you will not only be able to increase communication with the nonphysical world, including ETs, but you will also realize that your dreams have been an active communication pathway for you your entire life. Many Indigenous tribes, shamans, deeply connected spiritual people, and channelers are very comfortable moving in and out of the theta states and share powerful insights from spiritual sources.

Several exercises and resources are available to help you adjust your brain wave frequencies to theta. Here are a few:
- Do nondirected and guided meditations, including walking meditation and theta breathwork.[26]

- Listen to binaural sound beats, isochronic tones, and other sound techniques.[27]

- For those of you who want to know what frequencies your brain is operating at and learn to move it into theta states, brain wave wearable monitors can help you train yourself to produce these states.[28]

- The Close Encounters of the Fifth Kind (CE5) Contact app, developed by Greer, includes a step-by-step process for making contact with ETs. The app includes guided meditations, educational materials, and a networking feature to connect with others near you. The CE5 protocols use consciousness-based techniques, such as remote viewing, telepathy, and coherent thought sequencing.

CHAPTER SIXTEEN

CONNECTING WITH MEMBERS OF STAR NATIONS

BY MARTY RAWSON

Numerous protocols for contact are available through many teachers and mentors. To give you a practical example of such a protocol, Marty Rawson, a friend and colleague of mine, has graciously provided a protocol you can use in your journey to make connections with your galactic family. He has a practical and supportive approach to help you make your connections with celestial beings a real part of your life.

Rawson is an author and energy worker/healer who has had experience with the spiritual/metaphysical realms for his entire life. He integrates multiple healing modalities to help clients heal their lives and activate their connection to their higher self, the angelic realm, and Source consciousness.

The Paramount Journey to Unity Consciousness

Before we discuss contact with the Star Nations, I feel we must discuss the true bottom line of our goal: unity consciousness with our Creator.

We, as physical human beings, tend to be concerned about our physical world and the egoic attachments we have to what is familiar. However, clinging to what has been will not get us anywhere better. Connecting to Source is the single step that is vital for our own and Earth's ascension, *and* for making contact with higher-dimension Beings of Light—be they angelic or Star Nations.

As we witness the accelerating collapse of third-dimension structures, many of us feel compelled to "fix" what appears broken. This natural impulse, while well intentioned, actually diverts our energy from the most crucial task before us—realizing our own unity consciousness with the Creator.

Consider this fundamental truth: everything in our perceived reality stems from consciousness. The external world merely reflects our internal state of being. When we focus our energy on trying to repair failing systems, we anchor ourselves to the very frequency of those systems. Instead, we must elevate our personal vibration through the realization of our oneness with Divine Source. As I have stated many times, "Quit thinking like a human!"

Unity consciousness represents our natural state—the truth of our being that has been temporarily forgotten in the dense experience of third-dimension reality. This forgetting served its purpose, allowing us to fully experience separation consciousness. But that game has reached its conclusion. The time has come to remember our true nature as individualized expressions of the Creator's consciousness.

Our remembering begins within us. Rather than fighting against what's dissolving, we serve the highest good by cultivating our own direct experience of unity with Source. This isn't about escaping reality; it's about embodying a higher truth that will naturally transform our experience of reality. As each of us awakens to our divine nature, the collective consciousness elevates, and new systems naturally emerge, reflecting this higher awareness.

This process requires radical self-responsibility. We must release the habit of looking outside ourselves for solutions or waiting for external saviors. The transformation we seek manifests through our own consciousness shift into unity awareness. This means dedicating our energy to practices that dissolve the illusion of separation: deep meditation, heart-centered awareness, and conscious connection with our own divine essence.

As we achieve this unity consciousness, we naturally radiate a higher frequency that affects everything around us. This radiation of divine light does more to transform the world than any amount of struggling to fix old systems. Think of it this way: rather than trying to patch holes in a sinking ship, we're learning to walk on water. The old vessel may sink, but we've transcended the need for it entirely.

Many argue that this approach seems passive or irresponsible given current world events. However, the opposite is true. By achieving unity consciousness, we become channels for divine intelligence to flow into this reality. This higher consciousness knows exactly what's needed and orchestrates change far more effectively than we ever could with our limited human perspective.

The key lies in maintaining our own love and light regardless of external circumstances. This doesn't mean ignoring what's happening but rather choosing consciously

Remember that
we're not here
to save the old
world; we're here
to embody the
consciousness of
the new one.

where to place our energy and attention. When we consistently choose to align with our highest truth and divine nature, we contribute more powerfully to collective evolution than any amount of third-dimension problem-solving could achieve.

Success in this journey requires unwavering commitment to our own spiritual sovereignty. We must release attachment to particular outcomes and trust in the divine unfolding of events. Our task is simply to be the clearest expression of unity consciousness we can embody, allowing divine intelligence to work through us for the highest good of all concerned.

Remember that we're not here to save the old world; we're here to embody the consciousness of the new one. As more individuals achieve this state of unity awareness, the transition accelerates naturally. The old structures aren't meant to be fixed; they're meant to be transcended through the emergence of a new consciousness that renders them obsolete.

Let your primary focus be the cultivation and maintenance of your own unity consciousness. Trust that as you achieve this state, you serve the highest good of all in ways your human mind cannot fully comprehend. The time for struggling to fix what's broken has passed. Now is the time for remembering and embodying our true nature as divine consciousness in human form.

Making Contact

Personal experience is the cornerstone of divine truth. While people debate metaphysical phenomena endlessly, only direct experience reveals genuine understanding—understanding that becomes unshakeable once gained. Today, Earth's vibrational frequency offers unprecedented opportunities for divine connection, including contact with our Star Nation families.

I consider Star Nations part of the Divine because they represent civilizations that are millions—sometimes billions—of years ahead of us on the evolutionary path. Their accumulated wisdom will guide humanity through our current consciousness shift, a transition they completed long ago. The choice they faced, and we now face, is beautifully simple: Do we embrace the love, peace, and harmony of the light, or remain in the fear, hatred, and pain of darkness?

Even as humanity awakens slowly from its slumber, the Star Nations—true Beings of Light—have watched over and protected us from both ourselves and the dark forces that controlled Earth. These dark controllers are now retreating, knowing their time has ended. Consider this logically: if beings capable of interstellar travel intended us harm, wouldn't they have acted millennia ago? The truth reveals itself; the "invasion" narrative is the last gasp of fading dark forces trying to maintain control through fear. The light forces are here to liberate, not conquer.

The Arcturians, mentioned in ancient religious texts and Edgar Cayce's writings, stand as humanity's primary shepherds. Sanat Kumara, an Arcturian elder known as the "Ancient of Days," has guided Earth's evolution for more than ten million years. The Arcturian ascension manual, admired throughout the cosmos, contains just two profound words: "Be Love!"

Understanding Contact Experiences

Contact with Star Nations occurs across a spectrum of experiences, each uniquely suited to our individual readiness and soul contracts. The subtlest forms often come first—

synchronicities, number sequences, or recurring symbols that catch our attention. These signs serve as cosmic winks, confirming our awakening connection.

Dreams offer another powerful gateway to contact. Star Nations often choose dreamtime for initial contact because our analytical minds are quieter while we sleep, allowing clearer communication. Pay attention to dreams that are vivid and have messages. These aren't mere fantasies; they're often real interactions occurring in higher-dimension spaces.

Meditation encounters represent a more direct form of contact. As our practice deepens, we might experience distinct telepathic messages, visual images or light codes, physical sensations like tingling or waves of energy, awareness of a presence or being watched with love, or downloads of information or understanding.

Some of us experience physical sightings—lights in the sky, craft manifestations, or even face-to-face meetings. Remember that the form of contact you receive perfectly matches your current vibration and soul path.

Experiential Exercise: Sacred Space and Contact Protocols

THE PHYSICAL AND ENERGETIC ENVIRONMENTS

Creating optimal conditions for contact requires attention to both physical and energetic environments. Your dedicated space becomes a bridge between dimensions, amplifying communication potential. To prepare your space, begin by choosing a quiet area free from electronic interference. Create an altar with meaningful sacred objects, and incorporate crystals that resonate with cosmic frequencies (e.g., celestite, moldavite, phenacite). You should be sure that your space uses soft, natural lighting or candlelight and has comfortable seating for extended meditation.

Once you have created a physical space, you must also attend to your energetic environment. You should smudge with palo santo, sage, or your preferred clearing tools; set protective boundaries through intention or visualization; activate the space with sound (singing bowls, chimes, toning); and program crystals for specific contact purposes. It is also important to maintain regular energy clearing practices.

GROUP VS INDIVIDUAL WORK

Will you seek contact alone or in a group? Individual contact often feels more intimate and controlled, while group work can amplify energy and create stronger contact fields. Both approaches have value. The benefits of working in a group are an amplified energy field, a shared validation of experiences, multiple perspectives on contact, and a supportive environment for beginners. The benefits of working alone are deeper personal connection, clearer communication, the ability to work at your own pace, and more flexible timing.

PREPARING YOUR ENERGY FIELD

While the Arcturian directive to "Be Love" seems simple, implementing it requires dedicated energy work. Here's a practical approach to accessing and maintaining higher frequencies:

> **Begin with gratitude.** Focus on what you cherish—family, pets, precious memories. Picture them clearly and feel your heart's response.

Use this gratitude as a bridge to pure love. When your mind focuses on the beloved while your heart feels love, you achieve mind-heart coherence—a powerful state for connection.

Daily energy hygiene becomes crucial as contact deepens. Start your day by clearing your field with intention and visualization, strengthening your energetic boundaries, connecting with Earth's crystalline core, inviting in your guides and protectors, and setting clear intentions for the highest good. Your physical vessel requires attention, too. Consider increasing your water intake, reducing electromagnetic exposure, spending time in nature, eating high-vibration foods, and getting adequate rest and meditation time.

UNDERSTANDING AND PROCESSING CONTACT

Documentation becomes essential as your contact experiences increase. Keep a contact journal recording the date, time, and environmental conditions; your physical and emotional state; a detailed description of the experience; the messages or information you received; the physical or energetic sensations you experienced; and synchronicities following the contact.

Developing discernment will allow you to distinguish genuine contact from your imagination. When you are analyzing your contact experiences, notice the quality of the energy (usually it will be clear, loving, and peaceful), pay attention to physical confirmations, trust your gut feelings, and look for patterns and consistency. It is also important to validate your contact through shared experiences when possible.

Integration requires attention to physical symptoms (decreased energy or fatigue, sleep changes, appetite shifts), emotional processing (excitement, fear, confusion), mental adjustments (expanding beliefs, questioning reality), and spiritual growth (deeper understanding, increased compassion). *In other words, pay attention to your body and take care of yourself through the course of this shift!*

Building ongoing relationships with Star Nations involves regular communication through meditation. You must follow through on the guidance that you have received and express gratitude for the contact. It is also essential that you share your experiences appropriately and maintain high-vibrational practices. *Remember, these relationships are sacred and should be treated accordingly. Appropriate sharing would mean sharing them with like-minded individuals who would appreciate hearing your experiences. Sharing these things with those who are not yet awakened will, more than likely, not go well.*

INITIATING CONNECTION

To initiate contact with Beings of Light, use these three steps:

1. Extend an explicit invitation: "I invite all Beings of Light working within the divine plan to actively participate in my life. Guide me, protect me, and communicate with me in the most effective way."

2. Remain alert to responses from Beings of Light through synchronicities, intuitive thoughts, the clairs (psychic senses), and dreams.

3. Practice surrender to Divine Will, releasing ego-based control.

To strengthen your connection, use this daily affirmation: "Activate the omnipresence of Source/Creator within me, so I may be of divine service to Earth and humanity for the highest good of all concerned."

INTEGRATION WITH EARTH'S ASCENSION

Your personal contact experiences contribute directly to humanity's collective awakening. Each genuine interaction not only raises your vibration but also adds to Earth's ascending frequency. We're witnessing an unprecedented event—planetary ascension with physical bodies intact.

As contact increases, you might experience heightened sensitivity to energies, time distortions or timeline shifts, increased intuitive abilities, physical symptoms like ringing ears or body vibrations, and spontaneous downloads of cosmic information. These experiences are natural aspects of transitioning from Homo sapiens to Homo luminous. Your DNA literally upgrades through these interactions, activating dormant strands and capabilities.

For direct contact experiences:

1. Ground yourself in nature, especially among trees.

2. Connect your heart with Gaia's consciousness.

3. Enter a love-state meditation.

4. Project your consciousness above Earth.

5. Send clear location images with loving intent.

6. Request physical or ethereal contact.

Earth serves as the universe's Emotional University, now ascending into higher dimensions with us aboard. The entire cosmos supports this unprecedented transformation. As old systems crumble, embrace the change; these structures no longer serve our evolving consciousness.

The key to successful contact lies in maintaining consistent energy work while remaining grounded in daily life. Balance your expanding awareness with practical earthly responsibilities. Share your experiences with discretion, understanding that each person awakens in perfect timing. Stay grounded in nature, maintain high frequency through divine light visualization, and make contact through heart-centered meditation. When uncertain, simply remember the Arcturian wisdom "Be Love."

In Peace, Love, and Light, I pray for you all, the blessings of the Creator.

CHAPTER SEVENTEEN

THIS IS JUST THE BEGINNING

"The evolutionary fires that are beginning to flicker
and dance through our collective psyche may be our
wake-up call ... informing us that our true home is
elsewhere and we can return there whenever we wish."
—*Scott Guerin*

We covered a lot of ground throughout these chapters, and I hope you received some answers. However, just as I do, you may now have exponentially more questions than you did before and feel a little overwhelmed. So, what's next? Where do you go from here? And, how do you begin to sort your questions out?

One thing to remember is that time is not an issue. You don't have to fully understand all the dimensions, feel your direct connection with God/Source, adopt a unity consciousness, and have weekly meetings with ETs right now. Our lives are set up intentionally to be a learning process, continually experiencing new things and understanding Who we really are on our way Home. By design, this will take many lifetimes. So, we have all the time we need to explore new facets of ourselves and our place in the universe. We can enjoy the ride!

The first place to start is with what is in front of you. Start with one area or topic that you are drawn to and excited to explore. Each chapter lists sources and suggested readings for that topic. As you read or view them, you will be guided by your spirit team to the areas in your life that are most relevant to you at this time. They know your soul's journey and where you want to go, and they are ready at any time to intervene and assist you. All you need to do is ask.

One point to consider is that while exploring the different dimensions, alternate realities, and contacting ETs are exciting topics, the most important topic in this book is understanding your divine nature. God/Source is the beginning and ending of all things and all beings, and as a result, you are indestructible. It is where you came from and where you will return after your soul's journey. During this lifetime, you are a carrier of the Divine inside you, just like every other being in the universe. A large part of awakening occurs when you can embrace this in yourself and see it in others.

Finally, during an impromptu reading while finishing this chapter, I was told to emphasize that this book is just the beginning for many of you and that there are two other books to be developed. They will provide more details and guidance on several of these topics, as we all dive deeper into our journeys. Currently, I have no idea what these books would be about or what to cover. So, I invite you to be a part of the process if you would like. If so led, please contact me through my website (**angelintraining.org**) or Instagram (**@scottguerinauthor**).

REFERENCES

Chapter 1   Awakening to a Paradigm Shift

SUGGESTED READING

Copernicus, Nicolaus. *On the Revolutions of the Heavenly Spheres.* Translated by Charles S. L. F. H. Cohen. 1543. Reprint, New York: Modern Library, 2001.

Kuhn, Thomas S. *The Copernican Revolution: Planetary Astronomy in the Development of Western Thought.* Cambridge, MA: Harvard University Press, 1957.

Chapter 2   The Unseen World

NOTES

1. "About Abraham-Hicks," Abraham-Hicks Publications, accessed May 5, 2025, https://abraham-hicks.com/about/.

2. Esther Hicks and Jerry Hicks, *Ask and It Is Given: Learning to Manifest Your Desires* (Carlsbad, CA: Hay House, 2004).

3. Ibid.

4. Michele Governale and Ulrich Zuelicke, "'Spooky Action at a Distance'—A Beginner's Guide to Quantum Entanglement and Why It Matters in the Real World," MSN, October 2, 2025, https://tinyurl.com/46chc9w6.

5. Joe Dispenza, *Breaking the Habit of Being Yourself: How to Lose Your Mind and Create a New One* (Carlsbad, CA: Hay House, 2012).

6. Stacey Schmeidel, "Groundbreaking Study Affirms Quantum Basis for Consciousness: A Paradigm Shift in Understanding Human Nature," *SciTechDaily*, September 24, 2024, https://tinyurl.com/bdr249zy.

7. Carl Gustav Jung, *Synchronicity*, trans. R. F. C. Hull (Princeton, NJ: Princeton University Press, 1960), 104.

8. Nexus Void, "Carl Jung: Metaphysics of the Psyche," July 23, 2019, YouTube video, 22:03, https://youtu.be/fV0UkQAUsXI.

SUGGESTED READING

Hicks, Esther, and Jerry Hicks. *The Law of Attraction: The Basics of the Teachings of Abraham*. Carlsbad, CA: Hay House, 2006.

Schwartz, Gary E. *The Afterlife Experiments: Breakthrough Scientific Evidence of Life after Death*. New York: HarperCollins, 2003.

Chapter 3 Modern-Day Sources

NOTES

1. Charles Sanders Peirce, "The Fixation of Belief," in *The Essential Peirce: Selected Philosophical Writings*, ed. Nathan Houser and Christian J. W. Kloesel (Bloomington: Indiana University Press, 1992), 1:109–23.

2. Scott Guerin and Nichole Bigley, *Looking for Angels: A Guide to Understanding and Connecting with Angels* (SG and Audiowakes Publishing, 2023).

3. Mike Dooley, *The Great Awakening: Our Prophesied Transformation and the Attainment of Embodied Enlightenment* (Orlando, FL: The Universal Talks, 2024).

4. Dolores Cannon, home page of Dolores Cannon's website, accessed May 8, 2024, https://dolorescannon.com/.

SUGGESTED READING

Schucman, Helen. *A Course in Miracles*. 3rd ed. New York: Foundation for Inner Peace, 2007.

Walsch, Neale Donald. *Conversations with God: An Uncommon Dialogue, Book 1*. New York: G. P. Putnam's Sons, 1995.

Chapter 4   We Are Multidimensional Beings

NOTES

1. Michio Kaku, "Hyperspace and a Theory of Everything," Michio Kaku's website, accessed September 5, 2025, https://tinyurl.com/kzey96yz.

2. Alan Lew, "The One Most Complete Guide to the Spiritual Dimensions of Reality," Medium, last modified March 15, 2023, https://tinyurl.com/54u9azpf.

3. "Jane Roberts (Seth Books)," Amber-Allen Publishing, accessed May 1, 2025, https://tinyurl.com/5af823jh.

4. Matías De Stefano, home page of Matías De Stefano's website, accessed May 1, 2025, https://matiasdestefano.org/en/frontpage/.

5. Alan Lew, "Matias De Stefano's 9 Dimensions of Spiritual Reality," Medium, last modified November 22, 2022, https://tinyurl.com/au59436a.

6. Lyssa Royal and Keith Priest, *The Prism of Lyra: An Exploration of Human Galactic Heritage* (Scottsdale, AZ: Royal Priest Research, 1989).

7. Bashar, "Bashar Explains the Difference between Dimension and Density," July 2, 2021, YouTube video, 5:32, https://tinyurl.com/4hav55me.

8. Ibid.

SUGGESTED READING

Sam. "Density vs Dimension: What's the Difference?" *This Time on Earth* (blog), June 15, 2024. https://tinyurl.com/mr27zsnu.

Chapter 5

Experiencing the Spiritual Dimensions

NOTES

1. Barbara Hand Clow, home page of Journeys through Nine Dimensions, accessed May 2, 2025, https://handclow2012.com/.

2. Barbara Hand Clow, *Alchemy of Nine Dimensions: Activating the Full Spectrum of Consciousness*, 20th anniversary ed. (Rochester, VT: Bear & Company, 2011), 33.

3. Ibid.

SUGGESTED READING

Hand Clow, Barbara. *The Pleiadian Agenda: A New Cosmology for the Age of Light.* Santa Fe, NM: Bear, 1995.

Chapter 6   Piercing the Veil

NOTES

1. Raymond A. Moody, *Life after Life: The Investigation of a Phenomenon—Survival of Bodily Death* (New York: Harper & Row, 1975).

2. Janice Miner Holden, Bruce Greyson, and Debbie James, *The Handbook of Near-Death Experiences: Thirty Years of Investigation* (Santa Barbara, CA: Praeger, 2009).

3. Scott Taylor, "Into the Light: Meeting Your Guides," *Into the Light: Near Death Experience Meditations*, 2013, digital recording, https://neardeathmeditations.com/pagecd.

4. R. R. Griffiths, W. A. Richards, U. McCann, and R. Jesse, "Psilocybin Can Occasion Mystical-Type Experiences Having Substantial and Sustained Personal Meaning and Spiritual Significance," *Psychopharmacology* 187, no. 3 (2006): 268–83, https://tinyurl.com/4kxdjcwj.

Chapter 7   A Global Shift

NOTES

1. Asta Kallo, "Around 4 in 10 Americans Have Become More Spiritual Over Time; Fewer Have Become More Religious," Pew Research Center, January 17, 2024, https://tinyurl.com/47k9s9d5.

2. Daniel Lippetry, "16 Essential Meditation Statistics (2025)," Goleman EI, December 26, 2024, https://golemanei.com/meditation-statistics/.

3. "How Many People Meditate in the World?—25 Global Meditation Statistics 2022," Holistic Room, May 20, 2022, https://tinyurl.com/yxjbv6zp.

4. Neil Wakeling, "Schumann Resonance: Is It Changing?" Sound Intentions, April 25, 2020, https://tinyurl.com/44kycx9f.

5. Paul Ratner, "Is the Earth's 'Heartbeat' of 7.83 Hz Influencing Human Behavior?" *Think Big*, March 18, 2021, https://tinyurl.com/rzw3md4d.

6. Torrence Tremayne, "Astrological Environment for Spiritual Transformation," Tremayne Arts, 2024, https://tremaynearts.com/.

7. "Milankovitch (Orbital) Cycles and Their Role in Earth's Climate," NASA, last modified October 22, 2024, https://tinyurl.com/288u88et.

8. Giovana Armistead, "The End of Kali Yuga: What Lies Ahead?" Mythology Worldwide, January 28, 2025, https://tinyurl.com/cmysdvp6.

9. Dooley, *The Great Awakening*.

10. Frank Waters, *Mexico Mystique: The Coming Sixth World of Consciousness* (New York: Viking Press, 1975).

11. Eckhart Tolle, *A New Earth: Awakening to Your Life's Purpose* (New York: Penguin Group, 2005).

12. Dolores Cannon, *The Custodians* (Huntsville, AR: Ozark Mountain Publishing, 1999).

13. Ibid., 230–31.

Chapter 8   The Science of Consciousness

NOTES

1. David J. Chalmers, "Facing Up to the Problem of Consciousness," *Journal of Consciousness Studies* 2, no. 3 (1995): 200–19.

2. Ibid., 201.

3. Thomas Nagel, "What Is It Like to Be a Bat?" *Philosophical Review*, no. 4 (1974): 435–50.

4. Cogitate Consortium, Oscar Ferrante, Urszula Gorska-Klimowska, et al., "Adversarial Testing of Global Neuronal Workspace and Integrated Information Theories of Consciousness," *Nature* 642 (2025): 133–42, https://doi.org/10.1038/s41586-025-08888-1.

5. Muhammad Tuhin, "Consciousness May Come from Sensation, Not Thought, Study Finds," Science News Today, accessed May 1, 2025, https://www.sciencenewstoday.org/consciousness-may-come-from-sensation-not-thought-study-finds.

6. Dean Radin, *The Conscious Universe* (San Francisco: Harper, 1997), 144.

7. Masaru Emoto, *Messages from Water*, trans. David A. Thayne (Tokyo: Hado Kyo, 2001).

8. Radin, *The Conscious Universe*.

9. Paramahansa Yogananda, *Autobiography of a Yogi* (Los Angeles: Self-Realization Fellowship, 1946).

10. Eknath Easwaran, trans., *The Bhagavad Gita: A New Translation* (Tomales, CA: Nilgiri Press, 2007).

11. American Institute for Research, *Final Report: An Evaluation of the Stargate Project* (1995).

12. William Braud and Michael Schlitz, "Anomalous Processes in Human Consciousness," *Journal of the American Society for Psychical Research* 85, no. 3 (1991): 195–220.

13. Russell Targ and Harold Puthoff, "Information Transmission under Conditions of Sensory Shielding," *Proceedings of the IEEE* 62, no. 1 (1974): 4–9.

14. Darryl Anka, James Woods, April Rochelle, Erica Jordan, Zachary Dean, Daneah Underwood, and Ruman Kazi, *First Contact*, on Gaia, https://www.gaia.com/video/first-contact.

Chapter 9   Unity Consciousness: The Next Stage in Human Development

NOTES

1. Mary Schnorrenberg, "Unity Consciousness—What It Is and Isn't . . . ," Mary Schnorrenberg's blog, January 29, 2022, https://tinyurl.com/3nzj4ryr.

SUGGESTED READING

Chopra, Deepak. *The Seven Spiritual Laws of Success: A Practical Guide to the Fulfillment of Your Dreams.* New York: Amber-Allen Publishing, 1994.

LaVine, Rosey. "100+ Deep Shadow Work Prompts to Accept Yourself and Move Forward." Science of People, last modified May 24, 2025. https://tinyurl.com/c9n65xs6.

Ruiz, Miguel. *The Four Agreements: A Practical Guide to Personal Freedom.* San Rafael, CA: Amber-Allen Publishing, 2001.

Singer, Michael A. *The Untethered Soul: The Journey beyond Yourself.* Novato, CA: New World Library, 2007.

Thich, Nhat Hanh. "The Four Layers of Consciousness." Lion's Roar, accessed June 1, 2025. https://tinyurl.com/3u4ecfy7.

Thich, Nhat Hanh. *Transformation at the Base: Fifty Verses on the Nature of Consciousness.* Berkeley, CA: Parallax Press, 2001.

Tolle, Eckhart. *The Power of Now: A Guide to Spiritual Enlightenment.* Vancouver: New World Library, 1999.

Chapter 10   Our Divine Nature

NOTES

1. Sofia Marbach, "7 Zen Teachings from Thich Nhat Hanh to Live By," *Pachamama Alliance* (blog), April 7, 2016, https://tinyurl.com/4j7mum86.

2. Richard Rohr, "The Seven Themes of Alternative Orthodoxy," Center for Action and Contemplation, accessed July 1, 2025, https://tinyurl.com/2wxy99dk.

3. Amanda Williams, "How Many Denominations of Christianity Are There in 2024?" Christian Website, last updated January 14, 2024, https://tinyurl.com/329j9vbk.

4. Rev. Mary M. Mohan, "Workbook Lesson 160: I Am at Home. Fear Is the Stranger Here," *A Course in Miracles* Workbook Insights, Pathways of Light, 2003, https://tinyurl.com/yhz9nkty.

5. *Initiation with Matías De Stefano*, episode 1, "Unity," on Gaia, https://www.gaia.com/video/unity.

Chapter 11   Coming Home

NOTES

1. Rev. Mary M. Mohan, "Workbook Lesson 202: I Am Not a Body. I Am Free," *A Course in Miracles* Workbook Insights, Pathways of Light, 2003, https://tinyurl.com/2vrtrjy2.

Chapter 12　Do They or Don't They Exist?

NOTES

1. Courtney Kennedy and Arnold Lau, "Most Americans Believe in Intelligent Life beyond Earth; Few See UFOs as a Major National Security Threat," Pew Research Center, June 30, 2021, https://tinyurl.com/4w7cp3wy.

2. Robert Krulwich, "Aliens Found in Ohio? The 'WOW' Signal," NPR, May 28, 2010, https://tinyurl.com/bddz4rpk.

3. Eugenie Samuel, "Mysterious Signals from Light Years Away," New Scientist, September 1, 2004, https://tinyurl.ocm/yc2ucaa6.

4. Mike Welding, "UFOs: Five Revelations from NASA's Public Meeting," BBC News, May 31, 2023, https://tinyurl.com/583f43rb.

5. Luis Martinez, "Pentagon's UFO Report Finds over 700 New Cases, with 21 the Agency Could Not Explain," ABC News, November 14, 2024, https://tinyurl.com/2wyxzb9v.

6. *Unidentified Anomalous Phenomena: Exposing the Truth: Joint Hearing, before the Subcommittee on Cybersecurity, Information Technology, and Government Innovation and the Subcommittee on National Security, the Border, and Foreign Affairs of the Committee on Oversight and Accountability, House of Representatives*, 118th Cong. 2 (2024), 10.

7. Ibid., 12.

8. Ibid., 17.

9. Ralph Blumenthal and Leslie Kean, "Intelligence Officials Say U.S. Has Retrieved Craft of Non-Human Origin," The Debrief, June 5, 2023, https://tinyurl.com/2dd9w42k.

10. "UFO Whistleblower: 'Biologics Came with Some of These Discoveries,'" NBC10 Philadelphia, July 26, 2023, https://tinyurl.com/83vsr62f.

11. "Close Encounters of the Fifth Kind (2020)," Little Green Men Transcripts, September 20, 2023, https://tinyurl.com/96tyatkx.

12. Dylan Borland, "Testimony before the US House Committee on Oversight and Government Reform: Restoring Public Trust through UAP Transparency and Whistleblower Protection," September 5, 2025, YouTube video, 2:53:42, https://tinyurl.com/3dn5nd3u.

13. Ibid.

14. Erich von Däniken, *Chariots of the Gods?: Unsolved Mysteries of the Past*, 50th anniversary ed. (New York: Berkley, 2018), 88.

15. Graham Hancock, home page of Graham Hancock's website, accessed June 14, 2025, https://grahamhancock.com/.

16. *Ancient Apocalypse*, season 1, episode 3, "Sirius Rising," featuring Graham Hancock, aired 2022, on Netflix.

SUGGESTED READING

Anka, Darryl. "Books." Bashar, accessed June 17, 2025. https://store.bashar.org/books/.

Cannon, Dolores. Home page of Dolores Cannon's website, accessed June 14, 2025. https://dolorescannon.com/.

Carrol, Lee. Home page of Kryon's Legacy, accessed June 12, 2025. https://kryonmasters.com/.

Cori, Patricia. "Bestselling Books by Patricia Cori." Patricia Cori's website, accessed June 16, 2025. https://www.patriciacori.com/books/.

Hicks, Esther. Home page of Abraham-Hicks Publications, accessed June 15, 2025. https://www.abraham-hicks.com/.

Holt, Lyssa Royal. Home page of Lyssa Royal Holt's website, accessed June 15, 2025. https://www.lyssaroyal.net/.

Hoppe, Geoffrey. Home page of Crimson Circle, accessed June 15, 2025. https://www.crimsoncircle.com/.

Kennedy, Wendy. Home page of Higher Frequencies, accessed June 16, 2025. https://higherfrequencies.net/.

Marciniak, Barbara. Home page of The Pleiadians, accessed June 15, 2025. https://www.pleiadians.com/.

Selig, Paul. Home page of Paul Selig's website, accessed June 15, 2025. https://paulselig.com/.

Solaris, Debbie. Home page of Debbie Solaris's website, accessed June 17, 2025. https://debbiesolaris.com.

Chapter 13   So, Why Haven't We Been Contacted?

NOTES

1. Anka, et al., *First Contact*.

Chapter 14   Our Galactic Neighborhood

NOTES

1. Holt and Priest, *The Prism of Lyra*.

2. Darryl Anka, home page of Bashar, accessed July 20, 2025, https://tinyurl.com/2h8amhfp.

3. Nancy Thames, "Who Are the Lyrans?" *Time for Disclosure* (blog), April 18, 2021, https://tinyurl.com/bdhctjh7.

4. "Sizzling Planet Might Orbit Star Vega," American Museum of Natural History, March 24, 2021, https://tinyurl.com/455txcfb.

5. Holt and Priest, *The Prism of Lyra*.

6. Robert Shapiro, *The Zetas: History, Hybrids and Human Contact* (Flagstaff, AZ: Light Technology Publishing, 2010).

7. Adela Suliman and Paul Goldman, "Former Israeli Space Security Chief Says Extraterrestrials Exist, and Trump Knows about It," NBC News, December 8, 2020, https://tinyurl.com/y5mt9535.

SUGGESTED READING/WATCHING

"Are We GENETICALLY Modified Humans of SIRIAN Descent?" September 27, 2024, on Gaia. YouTube video, 40:54. https://www.youtube.com/watch?v=h0r4qjwfeNs.

Brooks, Julia. "Are You a Vega Starseed? Signs and Characteristics." Earth Soul Organics, June 5, 2024. https://tinyurl.com/mryd638v.

Bruntun, Susan. "Vega Starseed: Their Traits and Mission on Earth." Spiritual Nexus, March 5, 2024. https://tinyurl.com/3rrstu89.

"Galactic Family, an Overview of Genotypes." Iasos, accessed May 26, 2025. https://tinyurl.com/4bcjhczt.

"A Guide to Lyran Starseeds." Centre of Excellence, May 13, 2022. https://tinyurl.com/st672w35.

Hernandez-Oriol, Jane. "A Message from the Sirians." Medium, January 24, 2025. https://tinyurl.com/ywtrhd5s.

"History of Civilizations—Lyrans and Vegans." Crystalwind.ca, October 21, 2010. https://tinyurl.com/47n8nzkw.

Holt, Lyssa Royal. *Galactic Heritage Cards: A Journey through the Galactic Family Tree.* Tempe, AZ: Light Technology Publishing, 2010.

Kirsten, Charlotte. "Are You a Pleiadian Starseed? 21 Major Signs, Mission & More." *Typically Topical* (blog), May 21, 2021. https://typicallytopical.com/pleiadian-starseed/.

Lazar, Aeron. "The Sirians—Everything You Need to Know." Aeron Lazar's blog, August 9, 2022. https://tinyurl.com/2cdc88h5.

Lazar, Aeron. "The Sirians: 'We Made Our Prescence Felt on Earth.'" Aeron Lazar's blog, July 22, 2021. https://tinyurl.com/2rp8434e.

Lundin, Julia. "Are You a Lyran Starseed?: 15 Traits, Mission & Appearance." *The Spirit Nomad* (blog), accessed June 5, 2025. https://thespiritnomad.com/blog/lyran-starseed.

Lundin, Julia. "Are You a Pleiadian Starseed?: 16 Signs, Mission & Appearance." *The Spirit Nomad* (blog), accessed May 28, 2025. https://tinyurl.com/fdjcbtvd.

Lundin, Julia. "Are You a Sirian Starseed?: 10 Traits, Mission & Appearance." *The Spirit Nomad* (blog), accessed May 24, 2025. https://thespiritnomad.com/blog/sirian/.

"Lyran Starseed and Feline Starseed: Exploring the Cosmic Connection." *Flames Verse* (blog), accessed May 5, 2025. https://tinyurl.com/3tf7ch4h.

NASA Hubble Mission Team. "Hubble Refines Distance to Pleiades Star Cluster." NASA, June 1, 2004. https://tinyurl.com/bdd2j852.

Open Minds with Regina Meredith. Season 19, episode 6, "Arcturians, Pleiadians, and Lyrans, Featuring Debbie Solaris." Aired May 31, 2021, on Gaia. https://tinyurl.com/bdzydwb9.

Renee, Lisa. "Cradle of Lyra." Ascension Glossary, last updated February 7, 2025. https://tinyurl.com/5hysc58h.

Rood, Billy. "Chart of Progression: Earth's Galactic Family & Prototypes of Physicality." *FIFTY8*, accessed May 24, 2025. https://tinyurl.com/5n7shcdc.

Rose, Bee. "How I Discovered That I Am a Starseed." Medium, December 30, 2024. https://tinyurl.com/3bhwkceu.

Sam. "Sirius and the Law of One Connection." *This Time on Earth* (blog), January 12, 2024. https://tinyurl.com/mwh64krw.

"Some of the Core Concepts of Bashar from the Essassani Civilization." Iasos, accessed May 28, 2025. https://iasos.com/metaphys/bashar.

"Starseed Lore: Lyran Felines and Early Galactic History." Cryptic Chronicles, October 12, 2023. https://tinyurl.com/t56ctu9r.

Chapter 15   Preparing for Contact

NOTES

1. "Project Blue Book," Center for UFO Studies, accessed June 2, 2025, https://cufos.org/resources/project-blue-book/.

2. "Dr. J. Allen Hynek," Unidentified Phenomena, February 9, 2023, https://tinyurl.com/yck6bw6e.

3. *The Arc of Time with Ricardo González Corpancho*, season 1, episode 5, "Preparing for Contact," on Gaia, https://tinyurl.com/563dfduf.

4. "The 7 Classes of Extraterrestrial Close Encounters," Act for Libraries, accessed June 3, 2025, https://tinyurl.com/5ndknz67.

5. *Cosmic Disclosure with Emery Smith*, season 17, episode 9, "Portals & Protocols of ET Contact," featuring Ricardo González Corpancho, on Gaia, https://tinyurl.com/njf844e5.

6. Lyssa Royal Holt and Keith Priest, *Preparing for Contact: A Metamorphosis of Consciousness*, revised ed. (Flagstaff, AZ: Light Technology Publishing, 2011), 131.

7. Ibid.

8. Ibid., 44.

9. Carl Gustav Jung, *The Collected Works of C. G. Jung*, vol. 9, part II: *Researches into the Phenomenology of the Self*, trans. R. F. C. Hull (Princeton, NJ: Princeton University Press, 1969).

10. Holt and Priest, *Preparing for Contact*, 186.

11. LaVine, "100+ Deep Shadow Work Prompts."

12. Steven M. Greer, "The CE-5 Initiative" (presentation, Denver, April 8, 1995), https://tinyurl.com/59yzut48.

13. *CE5 Contact with Dr. Steven Greer*, season 1, episode 1, "The Science of Consciousness and CE5 Contact," aired September 19, 2021, on Gaia+, https://tinyurl.com/yd6v5d3t.

14. Steven Mr. Greer, "Making Contact: An Overview," Dr. Steven Greer's website, accessed July 14, 2025, https://tinyurl.com/mtnv87vy.

15. Barbara Marciniak, *Bringers of the Dawn: Teachings from the Pleiadians* (Summertown, TN: Bear & Company, 1992).

16. Barbara Marciniak, home page of The Pleiadians, accessed July 13, 2025, http://www.pleiadians.com/.

17. Lyssa Royal Holt, "Preparing for Contact: Seven Steps for Entering Species Adulthood," 2012, https://lyssaroyal.net/uploads/1/5/7/1/15716170/tran-pfc-7steps.pdf.

18. Holt and Priest, *Preparing for Contact.*

19. Jane Roberts, *The Seth Material* (New York: Amber-Allen Publishing, 1970).

20. Jane Roberts, *Seth Speaks: The Eternal Validity of the Soul* (New York: Amber-Allen Publishing, 1972).

21. "The Seth Material," Internet Archive, accessed July 13, 2025, https://archive.org/download/PdfsSethMaterial/The-Seth-Material.pdf.

22. Darryl Anka, "The Interstellar Alliance Social Experiment," Bashar, accessed July 13, 2025, https://bashar.org/socialexperiment.

23. Inner Shift Chronicles, "Bashar Reveals the Truth about Open Contact with Aliens," July 13, 2025, YouTube video, 12:34, https://youtu.be/FnbGEEbY-aY.

24. Holt and Priest, *Preparing for Contact,* 387.

25. *Cosmic Disclosure*, "Portals & Protocols of ET Contact."

26. Naressa Khan, "Theta Waves: How to Activate Your Brain's Hidden Superpower," Mindvalley Blog, November 5, 2024, https://tinyurl.com/359kh78x.

27. Kyle Pearce, "10 Ways to Activate Theta Brain Waves for Effortless Flow," DIY Genius, October 13, 2022, https://tinyurl.com/2e9kbtes.

28. Karuna Meda, "How to Manipulate Brain Waves for a Better Mental State," Thomas Jefferson University, November 26, 2019, https://tinyurl.com/njpcw9pv.

SUGGESTED READING

For further information on the biographies, publications, and activities of some of the prominent authors and channelers discussed throughout this book, visit their websites.

Darryl Anka: https://store.bashar.org

Dolores Cannon: https://dolorescannon.com

Lee Carrol: https://kryonmasters.com

Patricia Cori: https://patriciacori.com/books

Matías De Stefano: https://matiasdestefano.org/en/frontpage

Graham Hancock: https://grahamhancock.com

Barbara Hand Clow: https://handclow2012.com

Lyssa Royal Holt: https://www.lyssaroyal.net

Geoffrey Hoppe: https://crimsoncircle.com

Michio Kaku: https://mkaku.org

Wendy Kennedy: https://higherfrequencies.net

Barbara Marciniak: https://www.pleiadians.com

Paul Selig: https://paulselig.com

Debbie Solaris: https://debbiesolaris.com

Chapter 16   Connecting with Members of Star Nations

SUGGESTED READING

Kenyon, Tom. *The Arcturian Ascension Manual: A System of Physical, Emotional, and Spiritual Transformation.* Orcas, WA: Tom Kenyon Publishing, 2005.

Rawson, Marty. *It Doesn't Have to Be This Way: A Spirit Alliance.* Ogden, UT: Marty Rawson, 2002.

ABOUT THE AUTHOR
SCOTT GUERIN, PHD

Dr. Scott Guerin is an award-winning and bestselling author and educator with a passion for exploring the mysteries of God, the universe, and their relationship with humanity. With two master's degrees and a doctorate in human development, he has spent twenty-three years as an adjunct professor in psychology at Kean University. His popular *Angel in Training* series highlights society's shift from organized religion to spirituality.

Dr. Guerin's journey is documented in his books, including *Looking for Angels: A Guide to Understanding and Connecting with Angels, A Spiritual Journey,* and *12 Lessons.* His latest work, *Awkward Awakenings: Finding Our Way Home,* invites readers to awaken to their divine nature, their galactic heritage, and contact with extraterrestrial life. He includes exercises and meditative techniques to help readers access higher dimensions and embrace connections with intelligent life beyond Earth.

Learn more about Dr. Guerin at **angelintraining.org** or follow him on Instagram and TikTok (**@scottguerinauthor**) and on Facebook (**Angel in Training Series**).

CONTRIBUTING AUTHOR
MARTY RAWSON

Spiritual guide and lifelong metaphysical practitioner Marty Rawson empowers others to discover their divine essence and forge their own "Spirit Alliance." Through his book, *It Doesn't Have to Be This Way—A Spirit Alliance*, he shares transformative wisdom gained from decades of spiritual exploration and experience.

As the founder of Spirit Alliance, Rawson integrates multiple healing modalities—Ayurvedic practice, EMF Balancing, and Holy Fire III® and Karuna® Reiki Mastery (online and in-person)—and is a Melchizedek Method Level 5 facilitator. His unique approach helps clients heal their lives and activate their connection to their higher self, the angelic realm, and Source consciousness.

Rawson's mission is simple yet profound: guide others toward realizing their full potential as cocreators of heaven on Earth. His signature reminder to all seekers is "You are loved far more than you can possibly imagine!"

Learn more about Rawson on Instagram (**@marty_rawson**) or Facebook (**Spirit Alliance**).